MW00399093

# Finding Wisdom

# in the midst of

# Acute Loss

"Hold everything in your hands lightly, otherwise it hurts when God pries your fingers open."

Corrie Ten Boom

"I am your Best Friend as well as your King. Walk hand in hand with Me through your life. Together we will face whatever each day brings: pleasures, hardships, adventures, disappointments. Nothing is wasted when it is shared with Me. I can bring beauty out of the ashes of lost dreams. I can glean Joy out of sorrow, Peace out of adversity. Only a Friend who is also the King of kings could accomplish this divine alchemy. There is no other like Me."

*Isaiah 61.3*

*Jesus Calling,* by Sarah Young

# Why I Wrote This Book

Fear, horror, and resentment had burned me up inside! A helpless feeling that was utterly unbearable.

I see now my reaction was that of a frightened child. Unable to move until some big, loving, reassuring person cuddled me and gently told me it was all going to be all right.

This little memoir illustrates the time line of my belated 'growing up' through a horrific, unexpected misfortune causing severe loss that we're still living through.

Six years ago my life was one of enjoyed affluence; a carefree happy wife married 50 years. My husband Dean and I are empty nesters with well-adjusted adult children and were enjoying globetrotting, renovating the house of our dreams (complete with a dock and rather large boat), for our long anticipated retirement. Life was as perfect as could be.

But something happened dramatically changing the course of this life forever.

As a Christian of 60 years, my eyes and heart are being opened and I want you to join me in that. I am slowly learning the secret of being hopeful despite patches of acute anxiety; developing the habit of being expectant through what seems an eternally long wait; and the comfort of trusting God through that relentless 'fog'. Trusting that there is some kind of path that will be not just ok, but the best. Most important of all is finding the joy through being thankful for the chance to trust Him more.

Nan

# Hold It Lightly

## Contents

# INTRODUCTION

He is rat like and skinny in a gray ill-fitting suit. He trips like a tap dancer up and down our beautiful new wood stairs, rhythmically and loudly. A greasy, mousy shock of hair flaps over his beady eyes with each step. I wish he would trip and fall flat on his face. He is so rude and does not look at me even once. I seethe furiously inside. Here I am in my beautifully renovated kitchen, with gorgeous mandarin red counter tops, staring angrily at him, but it is as if I don't exist.

He never did ever speak to me through any of the tormented days that followed. He talked only to Dean, in hushed tones; long secret conversations usually out in the front garden by the garage; safely away from my listening ears I suppose. Nobody must hear. Nobody must know what is going on. The rat was on a vital mission and the last thing it required was a nicety! Nobody anywhere was to know anything until the appointed time. Dean asked, "How long might that be?" "Who knows?" he said, "as long as it takes."

I suppose there was a small element of relief – at least there was some action; they were at least doing something. But our hearts were in our mouths constantly as we watched and waited. My mind worked overtime besieged by obscenely overactive murderous thoughts. Resentment reigned supreme. And there were ghastly fear-ridden night sweats, tossing and turning, all followed by a false, beautiful hope that it was all just a bad dream.

There was a sudden urge to escape everyone around me. Nobody must know. It will spoil everything. They're 'onto them' but there must be no inkling of that. Don't speak about this. Better to avoid people all together. Fear loomed large, literally for our very lives.

However, even worse, I had a desire to run away, to slip past those inquiring, caring, curious questions from loving friends or neighbors sensing something was up. Do I lie? I have to weave a story to stop these endless questions. Yes, I must lie. It feels so foreign and feeble. If only I could yell from the rooftops the truth and get loving sympathy, loving advice, a loving hug and an "it's going to be alright". But, no, must not do that – not safe.

Rat stopped coming eventually; Dean's computer was returned; silence. Now what? This is a waiting game of some sort but what are we waiting for? Anything! Anything to get us out of this abyss, this hellhole!

# 1. MY 2016 LETTER TO A CURIOUS FRIEND

Hi there Judy - so much water under the bridge since we saw you guys! Wonderful news about the grandee!!

The story of 'us' is intriguing and long. Suffice it to say it so far has been a 5 - 6 year saga, and I've only been able to talk about it over the last 2 years. The most difficult part of the whole thing has been required silence. It involves a whistle blower, Dean, to the biggest financial fraud in Maryland in the amount of $278,000,000; an FBI case explaining the need for silence; four men found guilty, all now in prison. The chief perpetrator has been tried in Federal Court due to his holding out and Dean was a witness for the prosecution.

It was a Ponzi-type fraud, Madoff style, and we lost everything. It's a long convoluted story. We had to sell our dream home, not at a complete loss but in a bad market and had to sell so as not to go under - it took a year and a quarter. I held an estate sale with the help of five girlfriends and husbands, and our girls got what they wanted which we delivered to New York and Illinois by U-Haul, and now everything we have kept is in a 5x7ft storage unit in North Virginia where we were in our third house sit for 11 months.

We are now in our 10th house sit and it's a wonderful way to go when financially impaired like us. The trial is over and we await the outcome of restitution decisions. It's going to take several more months. We don't count on anything back as it creates too much pressure on ourselves and it'll never be what we lost! Also, we've learned that living in the moment is the only realistic way to go, so we can keep measured and sane and find some joy in life!

We belong to several web sites for house sitting and have lived in some lovely homes, met some fabulous people, and can't believe there are people out there who want strangers to live in their home and use their things! I would never do it!!

Emma and Christian are in Boston - 3 kids 12 - 8. Jess and Mark in southern Illinois with 3 kids 10 - 5. They are all superbly supportive and on our trips to various sits we fit in visits to them all as best we can.

We drive everywhere; have had some wonderful road trips; have covered all 50 states and love the variation in this amazing country. We've kept our sits to only in the States as can't pay for overseas travel. We bought a little 2003 Prius, which is wonderful on gas; we carry our two bikes on the back, a suitcase each, a bag of business folders, and our espresso coffee pot - bits of snobs about our coffee!

So, that is it in a nutshell, Judy! Haven't a clue what our situation will be in 2018 but hopefully will live to tell you, somewhere, about our tale in more detail. We gather you're now out on Waiheke Island permanently - looks wonderful and we well remember going out there with you. Haven't been home to NZ since 2010 and now can't see when that will happen. My sister and husband have kids and business stuff going on all over the world and we see them here often. In fact they're coming to see us in our next 'sit' in the Hill Country in TX in May.

Your jaw will be dropping. You asked for it so there it is!   Much love to Don and the girls from us


Nan

## 2. WHAT IS

Deano and I have arrived in Winnsboro, South Carolina, and sweating like dogs in all the heat. It's May 24th 2018, and the start of our sixteenth 'housesit'. We feel experienced, wily, ready for anything, and fairly nonjudgmental of other peoples' life styles. How can we be judgmental when those very folks, who under normal circumstances we would never have known, offer their homes to us in the most uncanny, open, trusting way, allowing us to use all their things as if they were our own?

As I've said to several friends, I would never in a thousand years use house sitters myself. It's something to do with invasion of privacy, control over my own property – not a loving attitude, I know, but then, we no longer own a house or have any property, so it's not even a consideration. And we are into our fifth year 'invading' other peoples' properties. We've become real connoisseurs of mattress quality, bathroom facilities and quality of showerheads, fridge sizes, hot water supplies, and spaces to escape each other.

Our very close friends offered their place to us in Chevy Chase while they were away for a couple of weeks before we came down here. In an embarrassed sounding voice I was warned that this was the first time they'd opened their home to anybody in this way, and please don't judge her if the fridge was not particularly clean. I know what she means – other peoples' eyes seeing and then judging how you keep house. A real threat! As I said, I would never put myself in that position. The funny thing is I seem to live in dread of the homeowner's return in case something is out of place, dusty, or just not good enough. So I simplify. I use the absolute minimum of their things. I write a list of where anything I move came from, photograph each room and almost die on the spot worrying that it's not going to meet the test.

I think this Type-A problem of mine dwindled just a wee bit after our fourth housesit in Illinois. Jess, our younger daughter had cleverly found a vacant place for us near them and we were so excited to be in close proximity to the family, and our beloved grandees for three months. It was mid summer and very hot, but the kids, just six miles away, had a beautiful back yard swimming pool, and we were going to spend the best summer all together. Turned out, our huge old house was flea infested on an industrial scale. They had no vacuum cleaner, so I bought a strong new one and lived at least twice a day at the end of it. I bought out Walmart of flea spray. I must say that place was in better condition when we left, and we gifted them the new vacuum cleaner on the off chance that they might use it.

And that leads me to say that in this present predicament of ours, we both always want to feel useful, doing something helpful, having purpose. The constant fact of being in strange homes, a new town, usually not knowing a soul to start with, makes it very easy to lose that sense of place and purpose. My comfy niche is gone and I have a desperate need to find something to give me a sense of belonging and "meaning". In fact this sense of place and purpose gets lost over and over, but I can make myself drag it back very slowly when I take the time to find the light instead of wallowing in the dark. A chat on the phone with an old friend, a real good book, or a rigorous, long walk, or some such thing helps. The light is there, it's just hard to find and hold onto sometimes. And I definitely have to force myself sometimes to '*get over it, honey*,' as my Texan girlfriends say. I have grown increasingly fond of the Texan attitude.

## 3. NOW, THEN, NOW

House sitting is our answer for 'the moment'. And 'the moment' is five years and counting. It's our answer to a dilemma we can't find our way around even yet. We wait and wait for some sort of way out, searching, and praying. We have learned together that 'living in the moment' is definitely a positive part of our answer. With it we can laugh together, encourage each other, and definitely find joy and beauty around us wherever we are. Living in the moment has a liberating affect. But I'm always wondering when the final answer or solution is going to appear, or become apparent. Being proactive in 'the wait' is a big lesson, trying to find my purpose in these sometimes dark and awful moments when I can hardly stand it any longer. Lord, help, please!

I want the grandees to at least be able to picture us somewhere definite and permanent in their wee minds. At the moment they see us just floating about in a car. "Where are you, Nanny, are you in your car?" James, 3, once asked me over the phone. The three oldest still miss our big, beautiful home on the bay - the Chesapeake Bay - but very quickly it won't even exist in their minds. Fin still says he misses it, but I wonder for how long? Will that memory be gone soon? Nonnie even lived with us for almost a year, along with Jess and Mark, while Mark was 'between jobs'.

We freely dreamed and changed the plain little saltbox house by the water into our dream home for family to enjoy. The attic we developed into a huge living space for the grandees to enjoy sleepovers together. Dean and I had gabled offices at either end so we had our hidey-holes but could yell lovingly over to each other and not feel lonely. We planned to retire in comfort and serenity, and sink into the mellow West River community happily, enjoying the ambience of the sunrise and sunsets over the water, and the atmospheric crab shacks. (Just watching South County crab pickers is an entertainment in itself.)

The big yellow and orange moon over the water, often huge, was just glorious, and the lapping of the water on the rock bulkhead around the property would lull us to sleep in our very huge bedroom now with it's own wrap-around porch. We would sit in our jammies in the breeze on the porch and soak up the vision over the water through the three rustling river birches Dean had carefully nurtured from 'sticks in the ground', as our unappreciative neighbor called them to start with. Those beauties had flourished into giants, and whispered to us in the moonlight. We called the property *Rangitata*, a New Zealand Maori name meaning "almost Heaven."

But that was then and this is now, and I sit writing in a carefully renovated old stone home that isn't mine in Winnsboro, allowing myself to revel in that escapist dream world of 'what was'. We've been here a week, getting to know the ropes, spending some time with the homeowners who are just lovely. They are about our age and are used to house sitters, but not with quite our story. Usually house sitters are in this gig for the free accommodation, for saving their pennies, for cheap international adventures – things I'm all for. But for us? It's just our best answer for now.

I've explored the ginormous new farm kitchen, rummaged in all the drawers and cupboards to find things, and have even cooked a couple of meals for all of us. It's an unusual feeling hosting the hosts who I've only known for two days, in their own home. They are due to leave tomorrow.

If truth be known, I've completely lost all interest in cooking, and have left every last one of my recipes

14

collected over the almost fifty years of marriage in our tiny store room in Reston Virginia, may be never to be seen again. Reston is where our very first long term house sit was. It made sense to have our 'stuff' close to us for those first 11 months. Also, Reston was only an hour from our old 'stomping ground', a very comforting fact being close to friends and familiarity.

The storeroom is 5x7 and stuffed full. That's what contains our belongings, those absolutely necessary things we refused to give up on leaving our 'Rangitata'. Probably, now, we could cut it down by half. The price of the space climbs frighteningly year by year and the importance of stuff we haven't seen for 5 years lessens steadily. We kept one set of dishes, some bedding, an expensive vacuum cleaner, a couple of fishing rods, and other weird and sundry things we thought were necessary in case we could suddenly settle again. I believe, now, that the old black and white photos in many boxes from childhood, early marriage and family life are the most meaningful. We're inclined to go to the storeroom only when we're in the vicinity and just to exchange seasonal clothing to suit wherever we are going next. Invariably we end up arguing over things that could be discarded or at least given away. It's all too much so it all gets stuffed back in there until the next visit. I know an old cast iron fry pan which belonged to Dean's Mom is somewhere in that storeroom. I used it every day and will take it to my grave.

However, in general, the kitchen has no appeal to me any longer. My kitchen was always my happy place where I could really relax and enjoy creating delicious meals. No, it doesn't have that appeal any more. It's someone else's kitchen, someone else's things, and it's no longer a pleasure no matter how designer or beautiful the kitchen. Dean is suddenly the one of us that has a new found pleasure of culinary creation. And that is an interesting point – he's a really good cook and I love that. It's proof that not all is lost.

## 4. WHAT WAS

We had arrived into our Bethesda, Maryland home in August 1991 after a dramatic move from New Zealand due to an irresistible job offer for Dean. He was asked to become part of a new and developing Privatization team with IFC, International Finance Corporation, under the umbrella of the World Bank, headquartered in Washington D.C. Phew! We reeled at the enormity of it all but were definitely thrilled with the idea. We had been living in my home country for thirteen years after an earlier huge move from Washington D.C. to Christchurch, New Zealand in 1978.

I call the move to Bethesda dramatic because of the age and stage of our girls at that time. They were 17 and 15, and had lived in New Zealand most of their lives. Life was going well on all fronts. The kids were sailing high academically, and entrenched in a frantic social whirl, along with a hectic sporting life. A lot of dramatic possibilities were cropping up for Emma who was becoming quite a big fish in a small pond with various acting possibilities in high school and also at university level. Jess was to be transferred into Wellington Girls' High from the private school she'd 'grown out of' and needed more challenge. The two would be at the same school just for Emma's last year.

As for me – I had all but completed a two year Teachers' College teaching diploma, had loved being involved in lots of community theatre, and was extremely enjoying settling into the most magnificent home we had recently purchased. It was perched above Kio Bay on a cliff, overlooking Wellington City, the harbor, airport, and the Remutaka Mountains in the distance, often capped with glistening snow. The house, originally a small post-war bungalow had been redesigned by the previous owner's American wife, and boy, was it obvious. Of course it oozed size, convenience, comfort and opulence, which went down very well with me. I felt very proud of this beautiful place with its two levels of floor-to-ceiling glass walls on three sides, sliding open to the elements and the sea breezes – perfection. And to think that Deano had made this all possible with the strides forward in his career in investment banking. This included a two-year secondment from the investment bank into the Beehive, New Zealand's Parliament headquarters, advising the Minister of Finance, Roger Douglas, during an historic moment in Government change there. A secondment occurs when a business organization offers, on request from the government, an employee to advise any minister in his field of expertise for a decided period of time.

Yes, things for us were going from strength to strength on all family fronts when this very tempting offer occurred for a move back to the States, and D.C., the 'hub of the universe'. And to cap it off, all moving and shipping expenses paid. Timing was awkward but had that ever deterred us before? There was not too much pining or sweating over the decision at all. It just seemed that this 'gift' was too good to be true. Of course it made sense! We felt the world was at our feet.

And so, as per usual, we excitedly accepted the challenge of moving through the hurdles as smoothly as possible. Hurdles being the sale and farewell of our prized home, the gut-wrenching passing on of our news to my bewildered folks, and then the loved rellies in Christchurch. Next was the completion of the copious paper work, the most time consuming being the complicated entry into the very different US schools for our teenage girls.

In the forefront of our minds was only the endless wonderful possibilities out there for us, and for the kids. It was like a strong, familiar momentum we couldn't stop. Dean and I had always noticed this about ourselves and laughed. We noticed that there was always the tendency to want a change after three years, be it our home, our location or job. Something triggered a three-year move. It was not ever truly planned, but we were aware of it and would chuckle, agreeing with my wonderful and also very forthright mother who would state often, "Dean is a very unsettled young man, isn't he?"

In fact between 1976 and 1991, when we made that move back to the United States we had actually bought and sold six houses. All dearly loved, in the end, but all replaced by something else for one reason or another. Size, location, suitability or just a change for the sake of it. Yes, unsettled. Actually, I have always loved houses, house hunting, nesting, creating coziness, color schemes, room arrangements. Houses talk to me.

So when we started hunting around the D.C. area I was in my element. And here we were, eventually in Bethesda, Maryland, just over the D.C. line, well and truly inside the Beltway, and in the best public school district there was. We were amongst the wealthy; the ex pats, a lot of World Bank and IMF types. The brainy. The anal. It was a very Jewish community too. It also had a big percentage of Asian ex pats, who all had brilliant children and 'tiger moms' aiming for the Ivy League colleges. Everybody lived in beautiful homes sprawling in gorgeous gardens. Every home a mansion but with a colonial flavor – that's what it was like, and even more so today.

The Principal of Walt Whitman High School, where the kids attended, spoke to the PTA at the first meeting of the year. His words still ring in my ears because of how well he captured the community. Dr. Marco said to the gathered crowd, "Many of you have complained that we give the kids too much homework. Well, look around you and tell me what you see. You parents are 60% Jewish; 30% Asian; and 10% other, many from the World Bank. So you tell me who is driving their kids."

And so, here we were, a block from Walt Whitman High School, on a dreamy little no-outlet, tree-clad street in the one contemporary house amongst colonials. And I set to, to turn our home into 'ours'. At the start I was a little overwhelmed by what we got for our money compared to our glass house on the hills overlooking the sea, mountains and sky in New Zealand. I felt very shut in, claustrophobic and not thrilled. But it was a charmed life we led, and with two renovations and a huge landscaping job completed in the twelve years there, it eventually bought about that sense of pride that had been missing.

I remember something I said with great feeling once to my mother who was visiting that I felt I lived a very charmed life and sometimes wondered how I'd cope if something traumatic happened, how I'd behave. We were obviously discussing something that had happened to a friend of mine in New Zealand and I was getting very philosophical. I've never forgotten that chat. Little did I know.

From that Bethesda house, we paid off with cash two weddings, one in Washington and one in New York; paid off with cash two lots of out-of-state college tuition. We travelled multiple times to New Zealand and many other places in the world, at odd times over the years treating our girls and their husbands because it was absolutely no skin off our nose. We also proudly entertained eighty plus guests for our fiftieths, and mine was a double whammy in that it was my U.S. citizenship party as well. We had huge British, USA, and New Zealand flags, one for each of my nationalities, suspended from our beams in the living room, masses of champagne, a band, and a barman, a boyfriend of

Emma's. I mean to say – nothing was impossible. We were doing well in the hub of the universe.

## 5.  UNDER THE SPOTLIGHT - AN EARLY LESSON

Our plan had always been to get out of dodge after both girls had graduated from high school but we didn't. We got entrenched in the community, and comfortably so. I even had a job with a Children's Theater Company. It was called Adventure Theater, the oldest Children's theater on the Eastern seaboard. I became part of an educational drama troop, acting and teaching either in our own theater in Glen Echo Park just down the road from our home, or traveling out to any schools that booked us. I actually performed in the 'Theater in the Woods' at Wolf Trap the out door performing arts complex in Virginia. It was all such a thrill.

In a totally different part of my life but at the same time, I had got very involved with a women's Bible study group called Creative Living International starting out as a co-leader and ending up as one of the traveling speakers. This appealed to me immensely, because I had been an aspiring actress all my life and always loved an audience. So, much to my delight, I was required to audition on film to become a speaker, and once chosen, was on tap about once a month to teach two different groups of about 60 women in the D.C. area, in McLean, Virginia and in Potomac, Maryland. I loved it. The groups were non-denominational, and not all women were Protestant or Christian. That's what I liked. There was a real mixed bag, but all seemingly well heeled and ever so stylish. They obviously enjoyed the founder's excellent studies, encouraging honest discussion sharing ways of applying the truths learned in the study. I loved the honesty between the women and the many elongated lunches afterwards at a local restaurant, carrying on stimulating discussion well into the afternoon.

I was raised by parents who lived their life simply and faithfully and who walked humbly with their God. Things of faith were part of the fabric of my girlhood family life, and it was lived so genuinely by Mum and Dad I never found reason to question anything. Although, as a little girl I remember getting embarrassed because we had Sunday rules such as 'no skipping or any games today'. I would wonder why we couldn't be a wee bit more like everyone else.

So, in my head I knew it all and, as a child, was steeped in the scriptures, prayer and family devotions every day before school. My father took a leading role in several Christian organizations. C. S. Lewis was my Dad's literary 'mentor', and I think Lewis' wisdom, and Dad's own diligent study of the Scriptures, kept his faith so balanced and sensible that I was never completely turned off, like some of my friends in our church congregation. Dad, to the utter dismay of some relatives allowed me to apply at the age of 17, for a whole year away in America on a student exchange, living with an unknown family. An aunt proclaimed to my distraught mother "you're throwing her to the dogs you know!" Dad was a champ.

He had a loud chortling laugh and we heard it often. My sister Ellen and I were raised on his favorite verses which were Proverbs 3: 5-6, "Trust in the Lord with all your heart and lean not on your own understanding. In all your ways acknowledge Him and He will direct your path." This became forever etched in my psyche.

There also did not seem to be a covetous bone in Dad's body. Material things were immaterial to him. He needed very little. We lived simply and frugally. Anything that broke in the home was fixed and fixed over and over until absolutely unusable. This was all much to my mother's consternation. She came from a wealthy background, and often reminded us that "Oh well, I married a penniless student. But I'll always love him". The one refrigerator ever owned by our family, purchased in 1953, had an eventual rubber band holding the handle together for as long as it worked, and that was until they left the family home in their old age.

Dad was quiet and happy in his own company. Not covetous of what other people had or of their life. He was happy with the simple things of life – a good book, a roaring fire with logs he'd chopped himself, with Mum right there beside him. He didn't grasp things tightly, or cherish anything to the point of desperation. He really 'held earthly possessions with an open hand' as I heard one guy once put it.

He would say to Ellen and me over things we fretted or alternatively got over excited about, "always be ready to give it up"; "hold it lightly"; and just "brighten the corner where you are." The 'hold it lightly' rings loud and clear in my head.

One memorable time Dad and Mum came on a first visit to a beautiful new home Dean and I owned. I was actually a little embarrassed because it was much more luxurious than I knew Dad would think necessary, and his opinion mattered to me. He was so gracious the way he wandered around very slowly with his head up high; nose slightly back, as he was prone to do. "It's beautiful, Woggits" he said, "but always be ready to give it up. Hold it lightly."  He truly lived by these principles.  As my life has unfolded, the benefit of this wisdom and seeing it lived out so authentically by Dad has been pure gold to me.

So, yes, with a humble and godly father like that, I felt I was the perfect candidate to be a Christian speaker! I had all this knowledge in my head that I truly respected, and I grasped eagerly onto the challenge and fun of holding an attentive audience in my hand. They would surely love my presentations, being the actress that I am!

It was within this CLI group that I learned for the first time the huge responsibility of passing on the untainted message of God's love and grace. I learned that the message must stand on its own. I was just the messenger. I had to get out of the way. It dawned on me that I was just a listener along with the other women. The very first time I spoke it was on Miriam, the sister of Moses. Having spent hours working out all my points, voices, and moves, early into the presentation I felt unusually awkward as I stood up there in front of around 60 women. It wasn't 'going over' as I expected. There were vacant faces, no smiles of rivited connection out there in the 'audience'. I realize now I was trying to entertain the whole way through, and nothing was working. My gift wasn't working!

In Mark 9 where Jesus miraculously cured the young deaf and dumb lad and the disciples were puzzled as to why they had not been able to do it, as they had cured in Jesus' name on other occasions. Jesus' answer to their question was basically that they didn't live close enough to God. They had been equipped with power but needed prayer to maintain it.

William Barclay points out that yes, God may have given us a gift, but in order for us to keep it alive and vital we must maintain close connection with Him. And this is for any gift. Without keeping close to the source of the gift, our Creator, we become just a mere performer, or professional using it for gain "which is a dreary thing," he says. There's got to be that profound joy using your gift, and that comes from knowing and believing you're using it for God.

I tucked away the truth of Barclay's comments where he warns of the absolute need to keep in close alignment with the Lord at all times. Otherwise, no matter how great the gift, that essential spiritual vitality along with humility has flown out the window!

I know now it's His good news, conveyed by the Holy Spirit and not my ace performance that moves minds and hearts.

I also love this quote from William Barclay in another part of his study of Mark, "There is a danger that a wise teacher must at all costs avoid... he must avoid all self-display. A teacher's duty is not to draw attention to himself but to draw attention to his subject. A love of self-display can make a man attempt to scintillate at the expense of truth. It can make him think more of clever ways of saying a thing than of the thing itself...A good teacher must be in love with his subject and not in love with himself."

Recognizing at last the danger and detriment, of my love and desire to entertain and be 'center stage', things got very somber in those sessions for several weeks because, with this newfound awareness I became increasingly scared to be myself. I suddenly realized that the way I was, with all my passion for being out front, was taking over. This teaching gig hit me suddenly as an awesome responsibility. I had to change in my attitude. It's not about me! The message is *for* me. I had to put myself in the back seat in order for His message to come through.

Slowly, I learned to be myself without ME being the focus. He wanted the focus on Himself. (Maybe that 'self control' fruit of the Spirit was newly activated!)

Very slowly, and ever so tentatively my old comic ways reappeared. Just a little more refined maybe? No, they were a little wiser! In the long run I treasured the time spent in study and preparation for those talks – Jacob being my favorite character – he was so awful, yet he would not give in. I found the "warts and all" stories very encouraging. Over the years I learned to allow myself to be quite vulnerable in what I shared with the women because there are lots of warts in my life, and there's a place for all of them.

It was with great trepidation I slipped into the shoes of Elizabeth Dole, wife of Bob Dole the Presidential candidate, at a luncheon hosted by the 'Women of Fourth', at the Presbyterian Church we attended. Mrs. Dole had to pull out suddenly as speaker, and there was a flurry of activity trying to find a replacement. I was asked - I knew they were desperate - and I took it on. What I came up with was my Dad's faith story, including 'hold it lightly', and of course also his love of Proverbs 3. It was an honor to do this. By this time I'd learned to make Truth, and not brilliant stagecraft, my priority. And to think that I was given these experiences in 'the hub of the universe'. At the time I would think to myself "Dad will be chuckling."

Dean, over this time was traveling internationally nonstop, with the occasional visit home to have laundry done, then off again. I got very annoyed with his tendency to be so hotel oriented; there was constantly a need for us all to keep readjusting our lives when he came home. But at least we were all very happy and 'going places'.

Deep-seated jet lag set in with Deano over these years and he'd fall asleep at the drop of a hat at the strangest times. However, slowly but surely, after seven years, he severed himself from the World Bank, and got involved with two or three different biotech start-ups.

The girls left the nest for college and marriage. We sometimes lazily searched for a new, more relaxing pursuit, whether it be a new house or a new job. Our plan to leave Bethesda seemed still to be on hold.

## 6. BOYS' TOYS

Then Dean found a boat! He had talked about his yen for this over a couple of years, and I must say my enthusiasm was almost nonexistent.

I think he had secretly been searching for a while because the need became kind of urgent and suddenly we were on a little exploratory visit out to a marina in Galesville on the western shore of the Chesapeake, twenty minutes south of Annapolis, and an hour from home. Someone at my gym had suggested there was a mine of information out there from friendly boaters, and it was fun to visit to boot.

What a day we had, the pinnacle being a lunch of blackened Cajun scallops at 'Steamboat Landing', sitting out over the blue water and looking at the many green inlets, some with scattered lovely beach homes interspersed with little old fishermen's shacks. Each had their own dock, surrounded by bobbing sailboats of all sizes, all so peaceful under the blue skies dotted with swooping, squawking gulls. Over our icy cold beers on that hot day in July 2003, we just imagined how wonderful it would be to live in such a beautiful and tranquil place.

Within two days we had bought a boat, a catamaran, 36 feet long and 16 feet wide. Deano read an ad in the morning newspaper and was immediately onto it in the afternoon. I have never been able to keep up with him – his relentless enthusiasm for new ventures, ideas, action, interesting people, with the general belief that 'anything's possible'. All forty-nine years of our marriage I have had to remind myself that this was and is the attraction I have always had to him. Always has been like this. He pulls me along and stretches the realms of possibility. Never says 'die' and all with such a cheerful demeanor. Can't resist.

But this boat was as much as I could take. Dean had not much idea of how to sail except for one two-week trip in the Bay of Islands, New Zealand, years before, in a rental 26 ft mono hull, captained by the 16 year old son of friends who joined us in their own boat. And this was all it took for Dean to be buying his own huge rig for 'trial and error' sailing that is, teaching himself as he went in the Chesapeake Bay. I was mortified! The owner offered us a year using a lift on his property on the Eastern Shore for free, a carrot to encourage us, and that was all it took. Actually, not a shabby carrot! So *Te Mozzie* became ours, aptly named by Dean because from a distance the unusually designed little catamaran looked just like a mosquito.

And so the sailing adventure started. We would go to church on a Sunday morning and plan on a nice sail in the bay in the afternoon. We actually got into a routine, which was fun. Most times out there'd be a glitch with the engine, actually, there always was a glitch with the engine, and I'd panic, way out in the deep water somewhere, and Dean would remain very quiet, ignoring the fuss I was making, and generally fix it, figuring things out as he went. We'd return to Bethesda exhausted but satisfied that we were back on shore and safe. Dean was obviously enjoying every moment. I really was not particularly in love with all this. Many times we were at the mercy of BoatUS, the Tow Boat rescue service.

One night late Fall we were forced to sleep under the sail covers for warmth in the cabin, with strong, strong winds buffeting the boat around its anchor. We were just seventy-five feet from our boat lift, the engine had given up and the owners were not home to tow us in – we felt very stupid, and green as green!

I did allow myself to get quite enthusiastic about going out overnight one weekend; gunk holing it's called. It was very soon after the purchase and I enjoyed the prospect of an eggs and bacon breakfast on the water, cooked in our little cabin, after a cozy nights sleep down in the hulls. I could imagine nothing better than the smell of bacon wafting over the serene, glistening, early morning waters of the Bay. I'd smelled other people's bacon from their boats and wanted others to smell ours! However it was not to be because we couldn't get the little two burner stove to work because we hadn't turned on the gas propane tank. I seethed all the way back to the boat lift, missing my bacon and convinced there was something else to fix on this blessed boat.

We did at last learn that the propane tank had a knob and when you wanted the gas to cook with you turned the knob. It was very hard on the knees kneeling down to open the little hatch to get to that knob. But at least we learned where it was, and at least that actually didn't need fixing.

We realized that the more we went out and experimented and practiced on *Te Mozzie*, the more prepared we would be for a longer foray into the real unknown. All through the time we owned her Dean proclaimed loud and clear his desire to do the 'Loop'. This foresaw a year, living on the boat, and traveling the Inter Coastal Waterway, rivers, lakes, and open seas around generally east of the Missippippi River. Experience wise we had mighty a long way to go.

As for our 'land' life we remained members of Fourth Presbyterian Church. Fourth was famous for an exciting and huge youth group, which for us was originally the big attraction. Dr Halverson, who went on to become Chaplain to Congress had been a previous minister here. He had drawn many politicos of Christian persuasion and their families to the church. Emms and

Jess were contemporaries there with Dan Quayle's kids. Jack Kemp often popped in to the morning service. Black limos would be parked outside with black suited security guards leaning all over them, awaiting their charges. The church was on River Road, opposite the Kenwood Country Club, and half a mile from our house.

I was pleased to be able to get super involved at Fourth Presbyterian as Dean was hardly ever around. I sang in the enormous choir, and also the chorale. The Director, Doug Mears was brilliant and very professional. He auditioned each member every year and ran a tight ship and it certainly showed. Doug was very encouraging to me and brought his children along to my shows at Adventure Theater, down at Glen Echo Park.

Seeing my interest in things dramatic he came up with an idea. He challenged me to write and direct a show at the church he called 'Fourth's Follies. The whole aim of it was to somehow coordinate selected music presented by the choirs and bands, children's included, during the year, into a dinner theater type production. This was all for the entertainment of anyone wanting to come, a type of outreach, I guess. I gulped and then grabbed the chance, showgirl that I was! I reminded myself that I had done similar things before and so took the challenge.

I wrote a script, devised a theme and became the center piece by writing for myself a strange little character part who leapt and jumped and skipped between the musical items bringing sense, order and meaning, injecting some humor, and also enabling me to sing with my own two choirs. It was fun, and went over like a charm. The tables were fully occupied; the laughter was from the bellies! The following year Doug asked me to do a similar thing and I was all set to go. However, it wasn't to be. I needed to return suddenly to New Zealand when my dear wonderful Mum became very ill with pancreatitis. Sadly, it took her and I was gone from Bethesda for at least two months.

A substitute was called in to MC the Follies. And that was none other than Cal Thomas, the Journalist and Fox TV Commentator. He and his wife were regular members at Fourth; they had taken part in my production the previous year and were a lot of laughs. I counted it a great compliment when I heard that he felt intimidated filling Nan Lewis' shoes. Ha! There was no doubt that at this stage I was on a roll, feeling on top of my game, and living very much the 'charmed life'.

## 7. THROW IN A NEW HOUSE

Dean and I were sitting through the announcements one Sunday morning at Fourth, turning our thoughts to a possible sail that afternoon out in the Bay. We heard the name of a friend and that she was in need of prayer due to illness. That was all he said. She and her husband were Aussies. He had retired after many years at the Bank, and church friends had introduced us soon after we first arrived because of both 'down under', and World Bank connections. Our kids were close in age, but apart from that we had not 'hob knobbed' much. All we knew was that they had sold their home in Bethesda a couple of years back, and had lived on a large trawler they owned in their first two years of retirement. This was something they'd dreamed of doing and so they did.

Unlike us, but prodded by one of those nudges you can't ignore, we scrambled around when we got home and found an old cell phone number of theirs. We had no mutual friends in common so there was no way to get a current number. Right after lunch Dean phoned the number and it worked. They were intrigued to hear from us, moved to think we were concerned about them and we learned she was to have breast cancer surgery the following week.

We were quickly invited out to see them at West River on the Bay where they had bought a little fishing cottage on the water. We were sorry to hear their concerning news and, yes we'd love to see them, and where were they? They were a few minutes around the water from a place called Galesville. We told our friends we had become sailors and were going to be across the Bay Bridge to the Wye River, sailing that afternoon.

"Take the long way home after your sailing", they said. "Pass the turnoff to Galesville, carry on to Chalk Point Road and see us on your way home." And so we did. And that was the beginning of our next chapter. Just like that.

On that Sunday afternoon, as we approached Chalk Point Road, off Muddy Creek Road, just passed the Swamp Circle Saloon, we turned left at fresh crab shack with the sign advertising "Fat Females $79". We had passed the Galesville turn off a few miles back, so we realized how close they lived to that 'Steamboat Landing' where we had eaten those delicious blackened scallops and surveyed the water and the inlets and dreamed of living there. Down Chalk Point Road, left on West Chalk point Road and right round to the water lapping the shores of the most idyllic scene. Curved shoreline, weathered docks, gulls and osprey winging their way over the sky, sail boats and masts dotted about, green grassy banks and bright garden flowers around little wooden cottages. No pretense, just quiet, secret perfection.

The cottage was around and on the other side of the point, and faced east over the water. We gasped with delight as we walked into the built-in porch and lapped up the panoramic feast for the eyes. Directly opposite the house across the river was the Chesapeake Yacht Club and marina with huge and tiny vessels bobbing about, and the faint sound of band music and laughter. Nice. "There's a house for sale next door" they joked, and we all laughed uproariously at the thought and went on to catch up on how things were. They begged us to come out next Sunday, post surgery to brighten them up and tempted us with an offer to all go out on the water in their runabout. Of course we would love it, and so I offered to bring a meal to share and a bottle of wine the next week.

After about two runabouts on the water with them over the next couple of weeks, and the fact that our year was almost up making use of the free boat lift over on the Eastern Shore there was the need to find somewhere to put the boat, hopefully the western side of the Bay Bridge. Here we were, girls gone from the nest, a very desirable home in Bethesda that we had meant to leave at least five years back. It was unbelievable that we had been in the same place for twelve years – not like us at all. Time to have a change and sell up? Why not?

We were sort of semi retired and would enjoy the fun of it all. Yes we would, so we bought the house right next door to our Aussie friends on Chalk Point.

## 8.  ALMOST HEAVEN?  ABSOLUTELY

It was a plain little brick saltbox built fifteen years earlier by the present owner and sat on almost an acre of waterfront property with water on two sides. We had our own bird-wading cove on one side, and on the front side a long dock, deep water, and everything perfectly ready to have a boatlift installed.

Although we still had our house to sell in Bethesda, we immediately set to and found a local South County design builder just down Chalk Point Road from our place who was very willing to work with us designing our dream home. This would include my highly desired wrap around covered verandas on two levels, completely new living space with dormers up in the attic, beautiful wood floors throughout, almost completely glass walls and sliding doors on two sides in the living room. It would be almost a total remake, an indoor/outdoor dream come true, a perfect place for family gatherings. This was going to be so much fun with money no object at all.

Our Bethesda home took time to sell but eventually we made the move, August 2003, just two weeks before Hurricane Isabel hit the Mid Atlantic – an experience that taught us how vulnerable we were out there to high waters, but we made it safe through with 8" to spare. Unfortunately our neighbors were not so lucky and had to rebuild using our same local builder. As a result, our renovations were unexpectedly slow in starting and the whole process was long. However, once we moved out to the Point there was no urgency, and we adjusted ourselves to the South County approach to life, which was easy and slow.

We loved the mix of red necks, and wealthy city retirees, shacks beside mansions, the call of the osprey teaching her babies to fly right over our house, the herons, imported swans, and big variety of ducks. The geese flyovers were something to hear and behold. Yes, we were not in a hurry, had all the time in the world and anyway being so tranquil meant more time to redesign even more of the house. Deano loved the creative ideas of the builder and he encouraged expanding them even further. The two men would wander around the property together and dream up the next step as they gazed adoringly at 'the project', gesticulating with their hands, obviously thrilled and totally carried away with all the possibilities. It was as if our supply of dollars came from a bottomless pit. At that stage we were confident all was well, and at last we were settled in the perfect place.

While all this was going on we got ourselves involved at St. James Episcopal Church, five miles away in Lothian. What a gem. Established in 1692, a true blue country tobacco church, many families born, raised, baptized and buried there. On an initial Sunday morning visit I loved seeing the burgundy and white robed choristers wandering between services amongst the ancient gray tombstones. There was obviously much love and care between the parishioners, so many of them had grown up together. We easily made some wonderful, lifelong friends.

After a few weeks I joined the choir, a group of varied ages and talent who just loved to sing together. It was an offering done lovingly and with great enjoyment, which to me made it perfect worship music. Michael Ryan, the Minister of Music, was the most patient, long suffering and good-tempered man with a glorious booming baritone voice. His claim to fame was singing the national anthem at the second Reagan Inauguration. Here at St. James he was sharing his expertise with this rather diverse little group of singers, always lusty and joyful whether that was the desired quality or not. I presumed Michael would be very happy to have me the 'oh so experienced one' join, with my theatrically true and quality voice to help them all along. But I learned very quickly, he loved and accepted everyone no matter the sound. He gave his heart to this choir, not ever expecting perfection. A good analogy of the Lord and us, his creation.

I looked forward to every happy Thursday evening we got together to practice. Being part of this Sanctuary Choir was one of my happiest experiences. Folks were in it to raise their voices in joyful praise together with no nerves about doing it wrong. Everyone wanted to be there. It was so relaxing. My voice vastly improved without all that nervous performance tension of the past.

With this newly found relaxed spirit I decided to start a study group – yes, to do some Bible study together. It was apparent there was no such opportunity at that stage, in the church. In fact I learned that there were women who went out to buy a Bible for this new 'fun' group they'd heard about. So with the Rector's permission, a group that I called, 'Goodness Gracious' was launched. Father Bill was very emphatic for me not to be controversial, to stick to the basics and not ruffle feathers. A new friend recently said to me, "the Episcopals have a very wide tent", and I know exactly what she means. I see love in action out in the community – not a group of talking heads behind closed doors agreeing thankfully they all have their theology straight. I felt that with their wonderful open hearts and eagerness to get going this was like a welcoming, nonthreatening, eager mission field.

We did some fabulous studies together on a Tuesday middle of the day, and if men wanted to come they were welcome. But the majority at that time of day were women. Deano joined me for two or three studies for couples in the evening as well. What a wide spectrum of thought was shared. No one afraid to speak up, ask questions, disagree, acknowledge new insights, - it was just great. Tim Keller's *The Prodigal God* was a highlight. Dean and I were beginning to feel an integral part of the place. It was a warm and wonderful, 'just right' feeling!

Our home improvements project did take a long time – two years in fact. It was a huge enterprise and we lived in the place the whole time, camping in the master or the guest room, avoiding the builders as best we could, and getting on enthusiastically with becoming an entrenched part of the community. It was a happy neighborhood on Chalk Point, with frequent 'happy hours' on each other's docks, or boat decks, enjoying the sunset and the honking of huge flocks of geese winging their way across it above us.

During this renovation process there was a four-month period where Deano decided to do a little work in Macedonia for USAID. It involved working with publicly listed companies to help them obtain capital from Europe and America. The job was divided into two eight-week blocks with a trip home in the middle. We both agreed that this was a good idea as our renovations were larger than expected, and this was a great chance to boost the cash flow. So there I was camping in a half-finished house, acting like a general contractor, overseeing the builders and ensuring they were doing their job. It was all rather fun, and with the neighborhood friends rallying around, meaning I had lots of company, it all went extremely well. Dean came home with masses of amazing stories, and was highly stimulated by being back 'on the job' and helping solve the world's economic problems!

Around this time, out of the blue, another very lucrative job offer arrived for the Deano. What to do? This smelled of yet another upheaval because it was in Philadelphia, a good two and a half hours drive from us. But the job was so tempting. One thing about it was that it had a beginning and an end. So with those simple boundaries we decided to 'go for it'! I was a pro at being 'solo', and these times alone with many reunions seemed to make for a very healthy marriage.

Dean would be interim CEO of the University City Science Center, helping start up life science companies to be successful. This organization, principally lead by the University of Pennsylvania, and established in 1964, had been the means of transforming gambling, drugs, and prostitution communities of West Philly into the most valuable commercial real estate in the city.

The acceptance of the job would mean commuting back and forth, but hey, why not rent a small apartment so both of us could enjoy the city of Philadelphia together from time to time? What a good idea, and so we did.

We secured a small studio on the fourth floor of a renovated apartment building down town on Chestnut Street, with a bird's eye view of the stunning, glassy Philly skyline. We fitted it out very sparsely from IKEA. Dean would train up, spend Monday to Friday and come home for the weekends. I soon found that the restaurants and shopping in Philly were to die for. They have a wonderful Daffys in Philly! So I'd sometimes drive up on a Friday and spend the weekend enjoying the sights and wonderful restaurants around the area with Dean. The girls and their families used it once or twice too for a weekend getaway.

The job lasted two years and then it was over. It was an unusual situation but one we enjoyed immensely. We returned to our tranquil life on Chalk Point having tucked another experience and much cash under our belt.

With the house done as far as we could afford we stopped and took stock of what had been achieved. A brand new very long dock, new boatlift and lighting, beautiful landscaping with outdoor garden lighting, gray river stone paths between ornamental grasses, river birches, crepe myrtles, and day lilies. Tulips galore, poppies, and masses of other brilliant perennials popped up in Dean dug beds, both front and back. Dean even installed a composter meaning we had better soil than anyone on the point. We sank into life in our 'Rangitata' with absolute abandon, relishing the peace, tranquility and beauty all around us.

Not always tranquility, not when the families came, but that was far better than tranquility. What a pleasure it was to have the room to breathe even when all twelve of us were together at once. It did happen occasionally. That sound of the kiddies' feet upstairs in the loft, calling to each other; Gilly tromping around in a Miley Cyrus wig and dress up high heels. The sailing out West River past all the neighbors docks towards the Bay, anchoring out, and diving into the water off the side; sprawling on the boat's trampoline, under the sails on a hot day as we swished along; the crabbing off the dock; the first fish, a perch caught by Fin; the cookouts over the fire pit on the cove's bank; the two bright yellow kayaks hanging neatly by the water, and the canoe where Patch played pirates and Fin taught himself to paddle alone. The sound of swans and herons fighting over territory; the 'slip and slide' and huge paddling pool we all fit into on the front lawn; the trailer rides out to the dump; the bird watching; the learning to ride the bikes on Chalk Point Road; and mainly, just the togetherness. This is what made us feel that things were almost perfect. Things had really come together. We had created a haven in a wonderful neighborhood for us all to enjoy. Rangitata, yes, almost Heaven. How much better could it get?

I made plans to redesign the kitchen. Yes, that needed improvement!

## 9.  A RAT IN THE KITCHEN

Around this time, mid 2008, we were so pleased and happy to have the space to put up our younger daughter, Jess, husband Mark, along with our wee eighteen month old granddaughter Norah, while Mark hunted for the elusive perfect job for him. In other words he was between jobs and they needed help.

They took over the loft above our newly built garage, carpeted and very comfy but without a bathroom. The bush outside the garage back door died slowly – poor Mark! The trek over to the house across the front lawn was the price they had to pay while with us. It worked well, though. It was a precious time.  Mark developed raised beds for us around the waterfront, while Dean, back to his roots, planned and dug and planned and dug and developed our ramshackle, untended almost acre into a garden paradise, almost Heaven. There was nothing truer.  We felt we had 'arrived'.

Mark is an artist and had helped Dean with some very artsy and sophisticated decals for our catamaran. Beautiful Maori design decals accenting many areas on the boat. She was called *Te Mozzie,* 'The Mosquito' – Mozzie is the colloquial term for mosquito in New Zealand. The 'Te' Dean added – Maori for 'the'. It was all a bit complicated when announcing the need for help over the boater's intercom radio. Nobody 'got' it, which meant numerous repeats until frustration usually set in. Once I heard the rescue guy say "what a stupid name". Ha! Each to his own. Mark, a sporty outdoorsy guy loved the cat, and Dean adored having such an enthusiast around. As mentioned earlier, I didn't fill that bill.

The three of us were out sailing one afternoon when a call came in on Dean's cell phone. It was a colleague of Dean's from the Science Center in Philly. He was someone Dean had got to know well and really admired, a brilliant inventor and designer of medical devices. He had an exciting investment idea for Dean to consider and wanted to pass on the good news and discuss it extensively right then and there. Of course it was not a good time with the wind howling, the boat rocking, and Mark, keen to keep going and me to get the whole thing over with! But, by the next morning Dean had learned about his friend's extremely good fortune and experience in investing in medical debt run by good, well-known and reliable family friends of his.

Dean was all ears because right at this stage in our lives the stock market was tanking and Dean had un-invested cash in the bank from stock in a successful company he had helped found. He needed to invest it outside the stock market. However, his reaction to this new suggestion was very careful – who are these people? Jewish. Family group. Hm. He looked at the whole scenario very diligently, spent countless hours on the phone researching the people and the product, meeting them all, talking it through with his colleague and he ultimately ended up enthusiastically investing. It was a very positive initiation, and after becoming familiar with the group involved, Dean found himself eagerly getting tied up more and more with it. He worked closely with everyone including the three principals of that medical receivables collection business. This all lead to a serious working relationship with Dean setting up a new company to feed money into the business. His enthusiasm and belief in the group was infectious and soon he had others, individuals and other organizations encouraged to invest.

All over this time I recall the endless hours Dean was on the phone or traveling again as in the old days. He loved the stimulation, conversation, and challenge of that necessary project to get his teeth into. I remember feeling a little miffed that he was not allowing himself to be retired enough. But then how much fun it was to open the envelope every month with the growing size of our returns - all very secure making. And for a while all was well. Life was sweet. Dean was happily occupied, avoiding the boredom of nothing to do. And I was busy with a Reico Kitchen Designer from Annapolis, getting my 'happy place' perfect!

It was after about a year and a half, in the early spring of 2010 that I started smelling a rat. Those envelopes I opened each month were not bringing the good news expected, and of course I queried this with Deano. He acknowledged he had become aware of a glitch that had been alluded to by the founders but it should iron out eventually – "Don't worry, Foof," an endearment, "just be patient". So I was-------- for a while. I just allowed myself to toss off the concern because that's the way I always was about such things. Any discussion Dean and I had about 'things at the office' kind of got blurred and shoved away because I must admit here that I was completely disinterested in all things financial, actually to the extent of total ignorance. It's something I'm not at all proud of. All I was concerned about was that our money was flowing in as I had been led to believe it would. My knowledge of Dean's profession and the whys and wherefores of investments, how they worked etc was absolutely beyond me. Any terminology associated within the realm of finance was totally out the window. I was utterly unmoved by any of it, and I never attempted to improve my attitude or do anything about it. Dean was the 'pro', the 'brain', he was looking after me, and I just kept redesigning my kitchen. In fact, I loved to make people laugh by announcing that I was just his 'kept woman'. Now I look back and cringe!

One evening Dean announced he had decided to take the train up to Philly the next day and meet over dinner with the key founder to 'iron things out'. Little did I know at that point that my husband was giving an ultimatum to the leader of the three founders. He obviously smelled that rat, but wasn't going to admit it to me.

Tension was brewing deep down in me, an uneasiness, but then I'm inclined to panic and Dean isn't. He's the 'pro'! He's always so calm, gentle, and rational.

Long since that memorable trip to Philadelphia, Dean has told me that he sat over a very expensive dinner and drinks, looked at all three straight in their faces and said "If you don't pay up I'll pursue you with the highest authority". Now, this just came out of his mouth. He had no idea what he would do or how he would do it, or who the highest authority could possibly be if it came to that. And you know what? Much, much later he did end up doing precisely that.

Slowly, after that, a creeping, seeping pall fell over us both as we carried on our lives. It permeated everything. The beauty of everything around us at 'Rangitata' turned a little dismal and gray. What was going on? Would our expected funds suddenly be released and everything be all right again? I'd rush to the mailbox in hopes, and Dean was mostly just a very quiet thoughtful man digging furiously in the garden. No returns to speak of coming in, and a slow gathering bewilderment.

The thought of the individual investors, and the international nonprofit organization Dean had brought into the start up made us both sweat! Creeping recognition of their potential losses was horrifying and unimaginable; far above and beyond our own funds at risk.

I know Dean wanted to keep me as free from worry as possible and I didn't want to badger him too much about what he thought was going on and I didn't understand anyway. I just continued to fret over the non-appearance of our funds. Everything got 'cloudy', 'foggy', and alarmingly frightening at two o'clock in the morning. I would lie in our sumptuous walnut, designer, California king size bed, gazing up into the dark and praying pleading prayers – "Please make it alright, please make it alright." Dean continued to sleep deeply. Something I envy him for - his ability to sleep at the drop of a hat. It made me a little resentful.

## 10. NEW HABITS, NEW PEOPLE

We resumed a habit around January 2010, of having an early coffee in bed over devotions together. I recall it began because we won the church choir prize at the annual Twelfth Night party after Christmas. The prize was a Bible arranged to complete reading in one year. The idea of the prize Bible was to keep it a year, sign it declaring you'd read it, and hand it back for the next year's 'winner'. I suspected at the time that most winners probably propped it on a shelf, dusted it off after a year and happily returned it signed and unread – something we very easily could have done ourselves. But with this new cloud over us there was a desperate need for some sort of 'rope' to hang onto.

The Bible replaced the *Washington Post* and we started reading the assigned portion for each day together and finished with prayer together for our families, for friends, and then finished with a plea for help. Now, we were both believers and active in lots of church group activities, but it took forty-one years together before we started this new, enlightening and valuable activity together and had our eyes truly opened. The winning of that Bible was no accident – reading it was a relief, a balm, taking us out of ourselves to somewhere else, which immediately helped. It's hard to explain actually. We had countless Bibles in the house but it seemed that this was a special gift.

We actually started looking forward to each morning's read, finding solace and comfort together over that green paperback Bible, a sweet start getting us aligned and braced for those awful gray days. Of course we weren't divulging anything of our concerns to anyone, not even our closest friends, and that in itself created horrible stress. But we were just hoping and praying the whole nightmare would go away, that the 'glitch' would just right itself. That what was ours would be rightfully restored and all would be back to 'right with the world'.

One morning Dean came in from a very long bike ride. He had started either digging long and hard in the garden or cycling for endless hours, chewing things over. He knew now there was definitely foul play within the company, and his anxiety was huge. More for those he had bought in as investors than for himself. In order to rescue their investment if he could possibly do it, he had knowingly put our own funds, everything we owned, at risk. And, of course they really were at risk.

As I write this, several years later I feel bad, and yes, guilt ridden at my lack of participation, my disinterest and ignorance about what was actually going on. Dean was making enormous, gut wrenching decisions by himself, with me just panicking madly about the money we seemed to be losing, and how unjust and evil and what about my kitchen I couldn't have now! I was looking at him and asking myself what on earth had he done wrong to make this be happening.

So, back to the bike ride. He arrived in after what seemed hours biking with a quizzical expression, but he was unusually buoyant. Very strange. It turned out that he had run into a neighbor. A neighbor we didn't know very well. All we knew was that he was retired and proudly drove a convertible Viper up and down our street. His wife was a real estate agent. This particular morning, unlike him, he pulled up beside Dean to pass the time of day. "How's it going?"

Dean got off his bike, and feeling desperately bleak he leaned into the car and let it all spill out to this man he didn't know. The neighbor casually admitted he was retired from the FBI, and "let's have a chat over coffee sometime." That was it. And he drove off. But to us both it sort of turned black to gray. In fact this was astounding to us. Completely out of the blue this man suggested a chat, and we felt we were being offered gold.

Every morning we would sit up in bed and get 'God aligned'. It helped. Whatever was happening was totally beyond us but it helped to admit it. We weren't really ready to make demands on God because we didn't know what to ask for. Together we had the need to put the whole thing somewhere. We each, of course, were contending with our own feelings about it all, and neither of us was particularly open about what we were really thinking. There was just a lot of silence, stunned silence and disbelief.

I know there are others of you out there who do know how we felt at that stage because trauma with its many causes brings with it horrific helplessness, hopelessness, and fear. Feelings that seep into your bones and permeate your whole being. There's no way to describe it appropriately.

Dean did not forget our neighbor's suggestion, our gold nugget of hope, and after a few days, over that cup of coffee, Dean described the gross problem that he had discovered. Our neighbor suggested that Dean write a formal Complaint. With the help of a lawyer friend in Washington, the three of them completed the Complaint.

From there, for several months this neighbor, horrified by Dean's story, worked his FBI contacts, and arranged a couple of meetings at the FBI headquarters in Baltimore. Would they take on the case? It all seemed a bit doubtful for a while.

However, in May 2011, the FBI launched the case and Dean became very aware he was now a formal witness. Immediately our world went mad. But how wonderful to at least have some action. We were suddenly thrown into survival mode!

An agent arrived at our house; hardly acknowledged me; ran up and down our stairs, mumbling in his cell phone. He asked if Dean would mind allowing them to copy his hard drive to accelerate email recovery. He asked us not to tell anyone what's going on – it would ruin any surprise element – and so the waiting game started. Waiting for the evidence to be found in Dean's records to nab those guys. It was a living hell for two years. The strain! We were not allowed to talk to anyone about what was going on. That was unimaginably hard. We had friends and family we longed to share this horror with – those who really cared about us, mainly to give us some comfort. However, we had to remain silent. Silence until they found what they were looking for. Excruciating.

Our neighbors didn't understand why all of a sudden we couldn't go out to dinner on a whim, take a weekend away with a group, or anchor out as usual. "What's with Nan and Dean?" It was awful, awkward, unreal and isolating. How were we going to get through all this or explain it? We felt completely paralyzed and penniless, swept down into an impossible bog we couldn't climb out of, and compelled not to spend anything..

I had this cut and dried awareness that I did not belong in the land of recreational shoppers anymore. We were in another realm altogether.

There was only one place we felt free to turn for that necessary off loading of our misery. We never missed those mornings of ours turning to the Lord over coffee. It became vital to our very existence. Who else could we turn to? And the first thing we did daily was to thank Him for sending this semi-stranger from down the street, our way. At least, at last, some hope.

## 11. SILENT SURVIVAL

In the meantime, we needed to carry on of course, but it was so hard. Ordinary life was carrying on all around us and I felt like an alien. 'In the world but not of it' took on a different twist. The huge mortgage on the house, once very manageable, was really weighing us down. We had no idea how long this FBI investigation was going to take. Our bank balance was frighteningly spiraling down but we were determined to keep up the payments, swallow hard, trust, and pray every day for quick resolution to all this. Yes – a quick miracle.

Night after night we would wake up at the same time, hold hands in the dark, stare upwards into the dark and just quietly mutter sentence prayers, desperate prayers, beseeching Him to do something. Please! Each of us also with our own silent thoughts, feelings, queries, and unvoiced things – too painful to expose.

Years ago I had picked up in the Giant supermarket little book called, *You're Late Again Lord*. In it I had learned that when waiting for answers we have to be active, proactive; – 'wait' is a verb. I remember I had sometimes used excerpts from the book to illustrate to women's groups with humor of course, truths about patience with the Lord when He seems 'late'. It all came rushing back to me. And so, one of those horrible dark nights, still holding hands we faced our looming crisis, chatted openly and honestly together, and sadly came to the realization that we must act. We must be practical. We must offer 'Rangitata' up to be sold. We agreed that this was the wisest thing to do at this time, and yes, the boat too. Offer 'Rangitata' and *Te Mozzie* up to be sold. It was harrowing, but also comforting to agree on this together and seal it with a prayer. I was learning how praying kind of balances out all the doubts, fears, and what ifs. Example, what if this is the wrong thing to do? In other words I did feel we had done all we could do and I simply trusted that our proactive decision would be redirected somehow if need be. This was a comfort, despite the sadness and horror.

In March 2012 a 'for sale' sign swung horrifyingly outside our gate, and now the whole world knew the Lewis's were leaving the neighborhood. The very awkward thing was, no one knew why and we were not allowed to tell them. That really played on our minds – how to deal with this? What to say? We were under strict orders to keep silent. In truth, I didn't have the 'why' completely straight, either. There were so many questions and queries I had, but when I broached this with Dean he would clam up and I really felt for him and let it be. It was one of those unspoken painful areas that didn't seem timely to bring up because I didn't know what it would do to us. I was trying not, at this stage, to 'lean on my own understanding', I guess.

The boat was duly advertised, and we worked furiously to get her cleaned up and ready. She sold surprisingly quickly to a couple from North Carolina who saw her as the perfect pleasure craft to take tourists, or other 'cat' enthusiasts out sailing, or overnighters to 'gunk hole' on or near the Neuse River. We were thrilled to think she was so wanted.

The buyers loved *Te Mozzie*. Later we learned they had dropped the 'Te' and kept the 'Mozzie'. I don't blame them – I thought that was a much better and simpler name. Dean couldn't understand why they would want to do that. They sailed her home to North Carolina at over 14 knots, a very high speed, and she proved to them how perfect she was for their touristic ideas. We were thankful, but even more, relieved. We had some cash to tide us over for a while, and that felt very good.

Now, it was crucial that we could share our predicament with the family, friends and neighbors, but somehow without explaining it. How could we keep within the realms of truth and yet not tell the whole truth?

The immediate neighbors saw the 'for sale' sign swinging in the breeze and were completely puzzled. They knew we loved our life here – it just didn't make sense. All so awkward. Just all so sad.

I found the letter below written to my sister Ellen, in New Zealand. In this I told her everything, despite the rules, and it was so hard to find words to explain to her. I was reluctant to send it. Ellen and Errold had visited 'Rangitata' at least twice over the ten years we'd been there, and enjoyed the whole beautiful life with us together with our girls and grandees. Sad and unbelievable.

===

**Letter written to my sister April 2012**

Hi Love
Lots of space and time between our connections!!
Hope you're all thriving and snuggling in for your winter!

I can't put into words what's going on here - it's easier to write it down in an orderly way so it's clear and you're not left dangling, wondering what's going on with us! In a nutshell we are reeling, and trying with all our might to keep our heads up. As you know by my call we have been subject to 2 different frauds - nasty, evil, somewhat embarrassing, and consuming everything we had!

We're at the bottom of a hole right now and a way out of it seems to be remote though things are still alive, legally, but only just, sort of just grinding along. I am out looking for ANYTHING to bring in some cash and feel silly not to have a career to fall back on - hence am seeking retail work of some sort, want to be close to home, so it's at supermarkets and fashion stores and I did go to 'Trader Joes' remember? yesterday, in Annapolis, as they are generous employers!!! Went into 'J Jill' too!

However the wheels turn slowly in this realm as well so it's all up in the air and I'll just keep going. Dean is overwhelmed and stunned, I know he's depressed and feeling sad and awkward - he will seek something seriously that will be much more help than anything I do, but is finding it hard to get his head around it which is natural. A "hump" he needs to move over and through. He's lost a tremendous amount of confidence. The going is tough for him and my heart just groans for him. I'm so thankful his heart is healthy!!! The boat is all but sold and that will be a relief. We're just hoping and praying that that will go through.

We had a neighbor, down yesterday who has been in Real Estate for 35 years, loves the area, and genuinely "gets" and loves our house and property. She's discreet and gracious, and we discussed our options in this awfully depressed housing market. It is likely the house will go up for sale, but nothing is selling! Have decided we can't have a negative attitude though, and will just test the waters. Renting is an option but much more expensive to us in the long run, I think. Who knows? We're just praying and thinking and mulling it over but will need to do something very soon.

We are keeping very involved at church with only a few people knowing what is going on with us. However, it needs to be out, and we need to trust more in our church community and their care and prayers for us. I think PRIDE gets in the way a lot and we have to guard against that and just trust God. We're slowly opening up to closer friends a bit - being wise about it though!

The girls are totally aware of everything, very concerned, loving and supportive, which is so comforting. Emms and Christian are still struggling work wise but grinding on, Jess and Mark are happy and settled. All the kiddies are thriving - just wish we had the freedom to see them more often.

May 3rd: Had church friends over to dinner last night. They have just been in the Holy Lands - sooo interesting to hear their point of view re the Israeli/Palestinian problems. Would LOVE to go there sometime.

Supposedly we close on the boat tomorrow. Dean has a conference with a Headhunter in the middle of the day. I was contacted yesterday re the Standardized patient opportunity using actors simulating illness, surgeries, etc in state of the art media rooms in order to test Med Students, and I'll go to an audition Monday week. It's quite good pay but not constant - great fun though - however, can't just look for fun!!

May 4th: Keep NOT sending this - hate to be so glum!! Today is settlement day on the boat. A busy day as they're coming up from North Carolina specially, and Dean has been busy getting it as good as he can. The buyer has seen it twice and seems to really want it. Will keep you posted.

Ells - I know your heart will be in your mouth as you read all this. I'm so reluctant to even send it to you. But that's not the way to be with my beloved sister!!! Just keep us close in your hearts and prayers - we are learning to just take each day at a time and any positive little crumb that happens I just say a la Dad - "Just hold it lightly" so we don't count rigidly on anything. So far so good!

Maybe we can talk in the weekend - we'll attempt to get hold of you at a time that suits us as boats and North Carolinians are about all weekend. It may not work out but we'll see.

Love you heaps, loads to Err
Nanny

PS Boat sold - Thank God!! New owners pottering around on it as I write, lugging all sorts of goods to it!

===

God is on our side and by our side, isn't He? I decided after that sale that yes He was.

Well, yes, we sold the boat, but nothing after that was exactly straightforward. We watched the 'for sale' sign swing backward and forward relentlessly. People showed interest and went away never to return. It reminded me of numerous auditions in the theater, thinking I had won the plum role, not getting it and feeling totally rejected. Why didn't anyone want to buy our house?

In desperation I ran around every day like a headless chook, oh yes, handing my days over to the Lord in the morning but forgetting almost immediately. Kiwis call chickens 'chooks'. Did you know that when their head is chopped off, they actually dart about in circles frantically for a moment, headless? In panic I frantically dashed into any local business within twelve miles of the house rattling off my dilemma and need for anything, please, to bring in some cash. Into supermarkets, clothing stores, and the local gym I went. All I encountered were startled, disbelieving stares – this elderly, perky little woman, up till now a known, regular customer in their store, an active member at the gym, suddenly very urgently not only asking but begging for help. The response was generally an awkward pause, round, wet cow eyes, a slow shaking of the head, and an even slower "sorry".

Dean, of course, was in a stunned, numbed state, working through untold emotional turmoil. I would fluctuate between absolute pity and sorrow for him, or annoyance and frustration, impatient that he wasn't running around frantically like me to find just anything to bring in some cash. After all, his decision had got us into this mess, I would tell myself! His resilience was amazing, but his determination to just 'be' and not be 'urgent' at that stage, often got my goat. Why was he not going to Home Depot for one of those jobs for the elderly we were aware of? Fear, anxiety, and horror were all pushing me into this frantic activity and frame of mind.

Next, I turned to the computer and started the search online for employment. But how thankless, lacking in 'soul', and hopeless that enterprise was. I was constantly reminded of how unprepared I was for this awful process, scrambling around to put together some sort of resume, not knowing how long we were to be in the area, the future a complete mystery. But I absolutely had to grab onto any sort of control I could, despite all that. And God seemed excruciatingly late…again!

There is a quote by William Paul Young of *The Shack* fame, I found in his later book *Eve*,

> "Mystery creates a space where TRUST can thrive. Everything in its time, AND 'timing' is God's playground. Trust me - being surprised by everything is so much better than needing to control everything".

Early this morning, here in our house sit in the heat of the South Carolinian summer we read together from our 'life-line' *Jesus Calling* more on this later, and I recalled what I had just written above about my problematic urgent nature Now, five years later, what we read today, is an absolutely priceless lifelong reminder.

> "Wait patiently with me while I bless you. Don't rush into My Presence with time-consciousness gnawing at your mind. I dwell in timelessness: I am, I was, I will always be. For you, time is a protection; you're a frail creature who can handle only twenty-four-hour segments of life. Time can also be a tyrant, ticking away relentlessly in your mind. Learn to master time, or it will be your master.
>
> Though you are a time-bound creature, seek to meet Me in timelessness. As you focus on My Presence, the demands of time and tasks will diminish. I will bless you and keep you, making

My Face shine upon you graciously, giving you
Peace."

"But as for me, I watch in hope for the Lord, I wait
for God my Savior; my God will hear me."
—*Micah 7:7*

"I am the Alpha and the Omega," says the Lord
God, "who is, and who was, and who is to come,
the Almighty."
—*Revelation 1:8*

"There is a time for everything, and a season for
every activity under heaven."
—*Ecclesiastes 3:1*

"The Lord bless you and keep you; the Lord make
his face shine upon you and be gracious to you; the
Lord turn his face toward you and give you peace."
—*Numbers 6:24–26*

Something unexpected did happen completely out
of the blue. A colleague of Deans from his earlier job at
the Science Center in Philly suddenly got in touch to see
if he would possibly be interested in a project in Nigeria.
The Nigerian government wanted to convert land and
buildings around Lagos Airport into a science center for
young entrepreneurs so they could develop their high tech
products. Would Dean be interested in doing a feasibility
study? Well, yes he would, of course!

So, in June 2012 Dean took a trip of only one week
to Lagos, but the fact that the project was right up Dean's
alley, and it brought in a little income, meant relief at
home, and actually a thankful heart for the few financial
crumbs dropped. The report was written, the payment
came in, miraculously one more months mortgage
covered – what next? We yearned for answers again. The
future was a total fog bank. And the 'For Sale' sign still
swung out there at the gate.

One morning I was mindlessly scrolling down lists and lists of employment opportunities, when I found a wee surprise. A job in jewelry store just a few miles from the house – who would have thought? I like jewelry. This could be fun. The extraordinary thing was that this was a family business owned by members from our church and though we didn't know each other, all my St. James girl friends knew them well. We lived in a semi-rural area and this was the place to go for all your gifts, repairs, and evaluations.

All of a sudden I was inspired and convinced that 'this was it'. It must be! I mean, all things point to the certainty of it, don't they? I jumped to and wrote a letter, wrote a resume that was in no way related to jewelry, found out when a friend who worked in there was on duty and drove at high speed to the store. There was my friend so I grabbed her and gabbled out my urgent need. Please could she make sure the owner gets this? She was open mouthed, electrified by the urgency. She had no idea of my desperate predicament and I'm sure this made her absolutely determined to find out what was really going on with Nan Lewis!

I got the job, 8 a.m.-6 p.m., two days off a week, some weekends. Close to minimum wage, and half an hour for lunch.

I could not believe what an enormous industry it was, and how competitive the sales women were, diving at an unsuspecting customer as soon as she walked through the door. There was so much to learn, and I made so many mistakes. Being thrown in to valuing gold and diamonds using scales, codes, magnifying lenses, and charts, I ended up with quotes that were  hundreds of dollars out on either side making customers either startled or very happy. There were watch batteries to install, birthstones to learn, custom neck, wrist, and ankle chains to design, antique pieces to value, displays to set up endlessly, and all the time racing to get to that unsuspecting customer first, ahead of the others. Commission!

I liked the gift wrapping and chatting enthusiastically to customers about their phenomenal taste in earrings. That was about my limit. I did not want to appear at Saturday promotions in fancy dress, all bubbly and "whoo hooing" while serving cake.

Within a week I knew that in my overwhelmed state of emotional turmoil, uncertainty, inability to concentrate or focus on anything, lack of sleep, house for sale, rat-like federal agents running up and down my stairs, I could not continue. I was going to have to let the owner down and pull out of the job. How absolutely awful and embarrassing it was. I know they hired me pre-Christmas to build up staff for the rush. Was I doing the right thing? Was I letting God down by turning my back on this 'gift'? Hadn't this whole amazing little job been the very needed thing? Hadn't it been His will for me? Now I would say, probably yes. Use what I learned. It was not wasted. Nothing is wasted. I had to trust more. It's all a mystery.

My mind floated back over other times I'd branched out on unfinished enterprises where I disappointed others and myself and ended up feeling a total failure. I'd once launched into a Real Estate course and become so overwhelmed I just bowed out. Was I doing this again? What a relief to hear wise words from my best bud when pouring out my heart. "Oh, come on, Nan" she said, "You can't bloom where you're not supposed to be planted." That really helped!

My darling mother would always tell me "don't just stand there, do something." This was her advice to me, as a child, to be polite and helpful when sleeping over at a friend's house. It was definitely in my wiring to start urgently darting about again to find what I was supposed to be doing to be helpful. But another friend and neighbor set me straight. "Don't just do something. Stand there," she said.

How extraordinary. Those words to me were the very necessary thing right then. I was compelled to do something to help save this great misfortune. But reflecting on it all now it was at that point that I suddenly felt the very best thing to help moving forward was just to stand there.

We got through the Holidays but don't ask me how? Our girls were aware of all that had happened, and were rightly shocked and speechless. The poor things. I mean, what can you say to your parents who, one day, tell you over the phone that they've just lost all their money? There are no words. That's what. Of course they loved us and tried to say soothing things and encourage us along. They called us every day to make sure we were ok, and in truth I suspect they were more stunned than us.

We spent Thanksgiving in New York with Emma our oldest and the family. Then Christmas we went out to Carbondale, Illinois to be with our younger daughter, Jess, and family. Six lovely grandees in all, three and three. What a blessing.

It's very strange living life within such a traumatic happening. Things are happening simultaneously on two different levels. The outward and then the real actual. The hullaballoo of family holidays with toddlers and children everywhere, carried on regardless, and they were a welcome distraction. It was a comfort to be able to enjoy the wee ones, to chat and discuss our dilemma eye to eye with the big ones, and to pray together for leading, wisdom, and help. We are so thankful the girls are in stable and committed marriages with spunky healthy kiddos. Just being able to hug and pray, laugh and cry together is always a tonic. Love soothes.

---

What will 2013 bring? It's a mystery.

## 12. GIFTS ON A PLATE

We entered 2013 in a fog, with two zip-lipped agents continuing to scavenge for prosecutorial evidence against the targets of the investigation, always looking very serious but to my annoyance, totally uncommunicative. I wanted some sign, any sign that things were on the up and up, that it was all going to be all right.

Sitting in our den's bay window one morning, fretting a little, sending up pleading arrow prayers, I flipped through a basket of DVDs. One was unopened, and I knew it had been there for years – maybe a special we had picked up, or a gift we had ignored? It was the British Italian 1977 Zeffirelli mini-series *Jesus of Nazareth*.

Actually, lately in those 'foggy' evenings, we had absorbedly been watching a couple of British TV series that somehow appealed emotionally in our state of woe. One was *MI5*, very thrilling and violent. We seemed to be swapping our 'violence' for a different violence. We repeated the whole series, all 83 episodes, at least once if not twice. The other was *Prime Suspect*, which had the same effect. Good versus Evil with good winning in the end but never without the most violent struggle. We found comfort in getting lost in the dramas and losing sight of our own drama for a short while. In his quest for justice, Dean, uncharacteristically sat alone and watched the entire *Girl with the Dragon Tattoo*, a Swedish trilogy with English subtitles, several times over. He watched late into several nights not being able to sleep. Far too violent for me.

On that morning in the den, I was in one of those 'can't move off this couch' moods and listlessly opened the DVD. It was only 10am but for the next six hours I sat riveted. It spoke to me like nothing else ever had. I was calmed, transported, comforted, and elevated. I don't know how else to describe it. For the next few evenings Dean and I sat together transfixed, oddly moved by this beautiful production. I believed this to be my desired 'sign' telling me all is well, despite everything. This was a gift. Last year great friends gave us a hilarious plaque for the wall with graffiti font, "If you're looking for a sign, this is it!" – I was waiting for a sign and here it was on this little silver disc. It was a sign to get out of myself and pass this on, this awesome calming message of comfort – Emmanuel – God with us. I couldn't keep this to myself.

Now the funny thing was, a few weeks earlier I had cancelled a new 'Goodness Gracious' study series at St. James. I was too twisted and overwhelmed and couldn't possibly imagine doing anything like running a study at all. Suddenly it hit me – Was I just going to sit here and mope? I felt swept into action all of a sudden.

With newfound energy I charged into the church office, announced that 'Goodness Gracious' was back on, booked the Church Hall for four Tuesday midday sessions, and got some lessons on running the apparatus and sound system. Not my strong point. My alert went out to 'come to the study over this Lenten time and see the life of Jesus in a whole new light like I have'. I think about twenty-five women turned up each week for an hour and a half of the movie and then discussion to follow. It was exhilarating and helpful looking freshly at the human experiences and relationships of Jesus with those around Him over the time of His life, death and resurrection. Some of His followers knew Him better than others. There were doubters, deniers and betrayers amongst them.

I know it was me who got the ultimate benefit from these meetings. Isn't that often the way? It was a combination of getting out there newly uplifted, but also being amongst good friends who I'd avoided. It had been hard to know how to talk to them when they were totally unaware of the huge jolt in Dean's and my life. However, just sharing our thoughts and sheer enjoyment together, laughing, crying, and learning, was the perfect solution. Gradually that sensation of 'all is well' permeated my entire self. What a gift. What a sign of His presence with me. I had been lifted out of that miry pit. Easter really held a whole new meaning - new life and real hope.

Dean and I were asked to share the homily at the Maundy Thursday Service that year in our beautiful wee church and I loved getting that ready. The most meaningful words of the ever gracious Jesus in that upper room to Peter, before Peter had even denied him "Peter, Peter, listen – Satan will get you, and for a time you will feel so wretched. But I have prayed for you that your faith won't fail. And once you have turned back to me, help and strengthen your brothers." In other words, His gracious understanding and love for Peter was so much huger than Peter's guilt causing mistakes.

Around this time another perk appeared out of nowhere. Sometime in June the Saudi government was referred by the Science Center in Philly to Dean. They asked him to advise on the expansion of scientific incubator facilities in three main cities. Of course he grabbed the opportunity and we were so thankful to be able to pay the mortgage once again. I did keep wondering how long these piecemeal, dramatic, paying work trips for Deano, could keep appearing. They were kind of mind blowing, and strange. But very acceptable.

And then it happened. We got an offer! An offer on the house. July 2013. A whole year and a quarter out!

Actually it was the second offer. The first had occurred away back in the first two weeks the house was first on the market. I can barely talk about it because it reminds me of the conflicted feelings and emotional baggage that ate me up over that time. When that first offer came in our kids from New York had literally just arrived, excitedly honking their way up the drive to stay for a few days. Dean was adamant that we were not ready to get out of the house as quickly as asked. I just couldn't believe it, or his reluctance. I immediately resented the kids being there right then because I couldn't focus, and we were under the most awful pressure, and why did this all have to happen at once? I resented Dean's black and white response to the offer, and I just resented Dean period!

I still did not fully grasp, or understand what had happened to our investments. My disinterest in all things 'business' caused me to kind of block out any attempt to do so. Maybe I just preferred to wallow, simmer and stew quietly with all sorts of mixed, difficult feelings of anger, hurt, and blame. To cap it all off, I was cornered at the mailbox by our very angry estate agent who lectured me, in all my inner turmoil, about the absolute benefit of accepting a first offer – there will never be another one to match it. And there wasn't. So, it took a lot of effort, self-control, and pleading prayers to get over a resentment I carried for longer than I care to remember.

But now, we simply had to accept this second offer. It was enough to keep us from going under, but that was about it. However, that in itself, after well over a year of waiting, was a great relief, and yes, we were extremely thankful. I became very aware of the phrase "Give us this day our daily bread" over that time. What we essentially needed but no more had been provided. Since that time this truth has been embedded deep in me forever.

We had two months to move out and nowhere to go. Still, there was to be no talking to anyone about our plight. It was uncanny just 'giving it all up to God' every morning, and then getting out of bed only allowing ourselves to think about that very day. It was the only way to keep sane!

I'm a very 'listy' person and now with the house under offer I created so many lists ready to tick off. We needed to strategize, prioritize, and get things done. It was hard to get a sense of order to start with.

There was very little equity in the sale, and we couldn't see round corners, so obviously everything must be sold. Dad's words "Hold it lightly" rang in my ears, along with, "Always be ready to give it up".

Dean found the idea easier than me. In fact, it seemed that our possessions were a millstone around his neck, definitely not mine so much! It killed me inside to think about all the loved bits and pieces we had collected from all over the world, everything in it's happy little nook to be enjoyed and remind us of this trip or that. We were surprised but not hurt at how little the girls actually wanted of our stuff. We duly delivered to them what they each wanted by the smallest U-Haul there is, and then were left with three floors and a huge garden of beautiful furniture to go.

Time was ticking, we had a month to go and everything was a complete fog bank.

What were we going to do? How would we explain this inevitable estate sale to our neighbors and friends? Where were we going to go? How could we pay rent? We need every penny there is to live on. "Give us this day our daily bread". I once heard a talk on line on "The Way of Trust" by a now deceased Catholic Priest called Brennan Manning. He said that the need for 'clarity' is the last thing we cling to. We desperately yearn for clarity. "Trust", he said, "is our gift back to God. It demands courage to have a childlike surrender and trust in the love of God and his mercy towards me"

It came, out of the blue, early one September morning. A very brief call from the FBI agent leading the case, saying four indictments were about to be announced.

We were free at last to talk!

Funnily enough, the secret out just freed us to get going. We had been so stifled for so long. The desire to wallow in peoples' pity was honestly the furthest thing from our minds. We seemed to only allow our experience to come up in conversation when it naturally made sense, and therefore there were some who never learned for ages, if at all, about it. We never wanted it to be the focus of things. I think it was difficult for lots of folks who did know, to talk to us comfortably; they were so stunned, sort of embarrassed, and lost for words. They didn't know what to say! But we felt extraordinarily free now to get on with life, and do what must be done. Thankfulness really does help perspective.

However there were other tensions. Over the last few years Dean had suffered with a mysterious prostate condition causing the need for a catheter at least nine different times. It usually happened during or just after long distance traveling, but had slowly got worse and more frequent. Around the next few weeks after the indictments was such a time, and it couldn't have been more awkward. I decided it was absolutely unfair. We had inspectors and contractors arriving every day for needed repairs, the one acre yard needing to be kept up, my old Kiwi high school friend and her new partner arriving to see us unexpectedly. I hadn't seen her for years. Of course I couldn't say no.

But, the most important and emotionally wracking thing of all was our carefully planned estate sale to be held over the next two weekends. Having never ever in my life needed to ask for help, I suddenly found I did. It was very hard for me. I know pride was at work holding me back. But I discovered that by just asking, a floodgate of love in action opened up, and obvious signs of relief in friends who were so desperate to help us and didn't know how. Now they could help, all because I asked. What a life's lesson. Six friends with their husbands who were very willing off siders, helped us plan the most wonderfully organized sale of all our stuff. I had researched hiring professionals and balked at the cut they took. No way, we decided, because we needed every penny and would do it ourselves.

One girlfriend led the way. She was a born organizer and thrived on stuff like this. She loved every moment. The team was to come in and join me for two days to price everything. I decided we'd have hot home baked scones, jam and cream, and lots of coffee to make it as much fun as I could.

But then, the week prior to the first of those weekends Dean had one of his turns. There he lay in state, up in our 'heavenly' bedroom, on the bed that we hoped would reap in thousands of dollars the next weekend. So with tensions running so high I was almost vomiting, we cancelled the first of the sale weekends and cancelled the Kiwi BFF visit. We nursed my man back to standing upright, back to removing the dreaded catheter after many days, and back, hopefully, to normal functioning yet again.

Later in that week the five girlfriends arrived to price, sort, and help set up the three floors into what to me felt like a design store. All our colorful, quirky, eclectic, funky stuff displayed beautifully. We actually did have fun. The girls couldn't believe how 'easily' I tossed off prices when they asked, and told little stories, without tears, about the bits and pieces. I honestly think I was super protected over that time – uncanny – Dad's voice "Hold it lightly", " Always be ready to give it up" - what a gift from my Dad. I had been given one amazing father by the Father Almighty. Thankful.

The Sale went without a hitch; every one of the five friends had their job, their husbands manned the outdoor spots including the boat shed and garage. Streams of people came, some we knew some we didn't. Both nights of the weekend we'd 'close shop', open a bottle of wine, turn up some favorite African music we loved, and wind down, just letting everyone know how much we appreciated them. It was actually a very happy time. Our neighbor friends got to know church friends, the combined group was helping us out and there was joy in that empty living room. The pervading atmosphere was love – no doubt about it – love! All of those friends of ours bought and took home things of ours, which we now enjoy seeing in their homes when we visit them – it's all a wee bit uncanny but makes us laugh with pleasure.

Of course there were the 'leftovers' that no one wanted to buy, much to my dismay. Little things, trinkets, small kitchen stuff, and so we donated it all to a wonderful local non-profit organization and it was gone, just like that. They came; packed it all on a truck and it was gone.

September 30th 2013, the last night in our house, we sat in the empty glass walled living room at a borrowed card table on two borrowed folding chairs, and marveled at the offer made just two days before by a neighbor, to go and stay in their house and get ourselves sorted out. They were off to their condo in Florida. He stood at our front door to tell us he'd just heard of what had happened to us, and there the miraculous offer was. I draped my arms around his neck and sobbed. Remarkable.

And so, Dean, with the merry band of husbands and a pickup, uplifted our last personal belongings in one load and deposited them three doors down our street, where we lived for the next six weeks in a state of utter bewilderment.

In that neighbor's house we faced east over the river as before, saw the same geese and heron fishing in the same marshes, watched the same osprey flying overhead, saw the same fisherman heading out in his little green runabout each morning, but it was all entirely different. We didn't own this anymore. But we saw very clearly what an awesome gift we'd been given over the last thirteen years.

## 13. THE REFINERS FIRE

There's nothing like being forced by unfortunate circumstances, or as Dean says, "being knocked off your horse like St. Paul", to look at your life, your desires, God, control, and hope, somewhat differently from before. Suddenly it's not just words in your head, it's Handel's 'refiners fire' literally consuming you. That's what it feels like. And it hurts!

## 14. LOVE

"Love is an incredibly powerful word. When you're in love, you always want to be together, and when you're not, you're thinking about being together because you need that person and without them your life is incomplete. This love is unconditional affection with no limits or conditions: completely loving someone.

It's when you trust the other with your life and when you would do anything for each other. When you love someone, you want nothing more than for them to be truly happy no matter what it takes, because that's how much you care about them and because their needs come before your own. You hide nothing of yourself and can tell the other anything because you know they accept you just the way you are and vice versa.

"Love can make you do anything and sacrifice for what will be better in the end."
From *Urbanthoughtcatalogue.com*

Yes, I think this is a pretty good definition. I haven't a clue about the origin but I'll take it. And I've decided it doesn't discount the very necessary times apart, which I know Dean and I need often, and we give those times to each other, mutually agreeing that it's time.

I'm not surprised at the different reactions from friends and others when they were first aware of our great misfortune. There was, and still is, usually a silence that I can read like a very large print book. I know I'd be one of these people too, with wide, shocked eyes that say,

73

"How could he lose everything?" "How do you stand it?" "What did you say to him?" "What do you feel like?"

And I'm sure the thought is there - "What would I do if it happened to me?"

So it's worth looking at more closely with you, because I've been 'forced' to do just that, look closely, in order to survive and still live to tell the tale. How could he? How do I stand it? What did/do I say? What did/do I do?

It was a very unusual, scary, confused feeling when first confronted with the news that everything material has been stolen from us. Gone. All of it. And, also knowing it could have been a much happier and easier story if a different decision had been made—by Dean! Yes, an error in judgment by Dean. I believed I had no part in this great misfortune at all. I was the 'kept woman'; I didn't make decisions in the 'keeping' realm, and we were suddenly confronting a great misfortune that was his fault entirely. That's how I saw it. I have a quick temper and could have slaughtered Dean right then, but something bizarre paralyzed me. In fact I was rendered utterly speechless and frozen. Truly frozen. I couldn't even cry. And, actually, same for Dean.

I should say here that what I recount below did not happen in a very clear sequence like ABC. It was more a slow development of happenings that I see now in retrospect and am just very thankful to God that with His help, over the months that it took, I was able to let everything fall into the 'tapestry' of our journey.

In truth I believe Dean had suspected the worst for a while, but now, as the truth became inescapable and dawned on me, he had not just his own horror, but me and mine to deal with as well. What has this done to Nan? At that moment he had no words. No words between either of us. No words of regret, apology, remorse or sorrow. Nothing. He was quiet, speechless, and hovered around me sort of waiting. Waiting for what? Probably for me to comfort him a little by saying it was fine, not to worry, we'd get through it together somehow, or something of that ilk.

But, with me it wasn't fine. A situation rife with horror, resentment, anger, blame, and fear was staring me right in the face, and wrecking my heart. It was excruciating. What was I going to do about it? I had always thought that over our nearly forty-five years of marriage we were a team. I thought we were truly 'one'. I know others saw us as such because they told us often enough. But it was a lie! How could he do this to me? Lose it all. Give up, in one decision, everything we owned?

The interesting thing at this point was that all my blame, anger, resentment, self pity, etc was directly pointed right at Dean, not at the perpetrators, not even at God. It was Dean, not them, who had let me down, put me and our best interests aside. I thought he loved me beyond all else, and would therefore want me to be secure and safe always. I was shattered and now absolutely without feeling. Still I could not weep. Frozen!

I guarantee many of you can identify with these feelings. In one way or another it is proved to us all either in horribly dramatic ways, or quiet little disappointments, that there is never ever 'self insurance' out of adversity. Aren't we all, inevitably, at some stage in our lives, confronted by an experience of loss, injustice, confusion or fear, that is utterly outside of our control? I felt at that particular 'realization moment' that the bundle I was handed was all of the above. There was absolutely nothing I could do to get myself out of this mess. And Dean had done it to me. Anger and resentment reigned. Frozen!

We both spent a few days being very silent. Silence is not my thing. Something made me be very adult and take stock calmly, which is also alien to me. So I was outwardly quiet and calm. Actually, I amazed myself at a sudden ability to shut up and think; keep things bottled up for a change. Looking back now I believe an angelic presence hovered around protecting me from myself, and protecting Dean also. It really was quite remarkable. You see, I understand now that right then I had to just 'stand right there'. I had to stand to 'be', and not to 'do' yet.

So there we were in this state of disbelief over the great misfortune, and I was sending up quick little arrow 'help me' prayers for some clarity, and assurance that I wasn't going to lose it altogether. See, at times such as these, to be absolutely honest, dark thoughts start accumulating, don't they? I'd rather be dead. I'll just leave. I'll end this right away to get relief. I feel so sick I can't stand it. I hope I wake up and this is all a nightmare!

Hateful resentment was building and in bed over the next nights I'd find myself lying and facing the opposite way from Dean, not touching, all in silence and bewilderment and hurt. I could feel the hurt and resentment choking me. New, horrible poisonous feelings hovered. How was I going to survive? "Please help me see Dean through new eyes" I pleaded into the dark. I think it must have been a realization that the anger could only be relieved by looking at Dean without it, or something like that. I don't really understand, but that's what I asked. A strange thing to ask when all I thought was he was the one to blame.

This was a constant nightly battle for a while but over those nights and days I found I was able to contemplate our life together, still silent on the whole, and still absolutely stunned.

Every now and then I would find myself pitying Dean a little, realizing how ghastly he must feel. But, of course, there was no intention to ease it for him. I didn't really know how to be or act. The horror and resentment stayed there festering. I would continue to quietly plead with Jesus to help me look at Dean anew, not the situation. Dean! And then I'd wonder why I did that. The two of us didn't really address the subject point blank at all. Like deer in the headlights we were just helplessly stunned and directionless.

This guy of mine after all these years of adventure, of success, and lots of laughter, was hurting so badly – of course I knew that and could feel it. The poor, poor man had suffered the biggest crisis which for him, in his line of work, must be such an awful embarrassment. His pride must be down in the deepest pit, his guilt as to what this all meant to me, to our girls, to our friends, to his family, who considered him almost royalty because of his successes. But probably mainly to all his colleagues and connections in business over the years. This was just awful. Awful for him. How could he stand it?

Dean, who I'd known and loved for fifty years – such an honest, genuine, inspired, inquiring, enthusiastic, persistent yet gentle man. I had loved him from the beginning. We had met when we were seventeen. His ability to bring me along with him in his endeavors with humor and a lot of fun-filled cajoling, which I needed very often. He saw things in me I hadn't found for myself and was so encouraging and inspiring. I found his constant new ideas enticing and irresistible, but I must admit would roll my eyes a lot and sigh, exhausted by his energy. Nothing was proved impossible until tried with Dean, and always with a chuckle. We were real mates, never really holding anything back from each other, until this horror. It was, or had been, a very honest relationship.

We had produced two beautiful girls, who had eventually moved admirably into mature adult lives. They had a great hold on life, great humor, and deep love for their own husbands and children, our darling grandchildren. Our girls are tenacious, loving and kind. In our own ways we had achieved this together and are proud of them.

Underlying everything else, I thought, was Dean's tremendous ability to bring out the other person and to be genuinely interested in what was going on in their lives. He was so quick to help, to offer encouragement, and to be genuinely involved with them. He always put others first. I loved him for that. I truly admired him. He has touched many lives with his generosity and selfless, enthusiastic ways.

Yes, I did hurt for him deeply.

He'd now done something that I couldn't grasp, and now everything was ruined forever. I had never understood anything in Dean's work world. I didn't want to understand. I just blocked off or glazed over when the subject of work ever came up. It didn't remotely interest me. I left him to it and went off into my own little world. Dean had always said to me that he believed I earned half his salary. I happily held onto that thought and though always rather frugal, never gave the money he earned a thought. As long as it was there to spend, I guess!

Perhaps if I had been a little more engaged, and shown more interest in the huge load and urgent decisions he was making, things may have turned out differently. I became very aware that I was not only hurting for me, but hurting for him. Yes, love is there. This thought hit me like a rock. My newly sour view of Dean was diluted a little and I asked God for forgiveness there in the dark. Then I set about to try to forgive myself a little.

"For love is as strong as death, passion is as unrelenting as Sheol.
Its flames burst forth, it is a blazing flame.
Surging waters cannot quench love;
Floodwaters cannot overflow it.
If someone were to offer all his possessions to buy love,
The offer would be utterly despised."

*Song of Solomon 8: 6-7*

Strong, unrelenting, blazing. This description of love in the Song of Songs does make me laugh a little. I realize that true love wins out when it's real, but it still doesn't get rid of the baggage and all those feelings and hurts that lurk around! I think that is why Alexander Pope's line 'to err is human to forgive divine' really resonates. I had pleaded for help, "help me see Dean through new eyes", and here it was. The mysterious Divine help assuring me that I still loved Dean. We were a team and I needed to address my role in all this.

I pondered this awsome ability I suddenly had to be still, silent, and patient as I pleaded for help. I was seeing Dean slightly differently. So I thanked God for the relief, and the impetus to move forward, and slept well for the first time in ages.

So many times over these last few years, the truth of Paul's statement in Ephesians is proved over and over. Here it is from *The Message:* "God can do anything, you know – far more than you could ever imagine or guess or request in your wildest dreams! He does it not by pushing us around but by working within us, his Spirit deeply and gently within us."

But despite all that, in my mind Dean had nonetheless screwed up bigly! Blame and resentment still reigned regardless. I had to move on and out from that somehow, with God's help. I didn't know how to do it, and, of course, in that wallowing, self-pitying way, I didn't want to do it. It involved forgiveness. Love and forgiveness go together.

I have discovered that love and forgiveness are inextricably joined. Awkward!

## 15. FORGIVE

*"Start by doing what is necessary; then do what's possible; and suddenly you are doing the impossible."*

St. Francis of Assisi

### The Necessary

I just love this quote from St. Francis. It makes sense. And it's reasonable. My necessary thing was to call out to Jesus, reach out, and plead for His help to do something that I didn't understand but was urged to do it. All I knew was that in my eyes it was all Dean's fault! "Help me see Dean through new eyes". I think I did that over and over in panic because there was nowhere else to go, I didn't know what else to say, and felt completely powerless and certainly couldn't do it for myself. I understand now that when I reached out into the dark pleading to see Dean through new eyes I was being lead by the spirit to see not just Dean but the whole great misfortune through God's eyes. My new eyes – His perspective.

"Meanwhile, the moment we get tired in the waiting, God's Spirit is right alongside helping us along. If we don't know how or what to pray, it doesn't matter. He does our praying in and for us, making prayer out of our wordless sighs, our aching groans. He knows us far better than we know ourselves, knows our pregnant condition, and keeps us present before God. That's why we can be so sure that every detail in our lives of love for God is worked into something good." *Romans 8: 26-27*

It helped calm me immediately. And the source of all Love, Love itself, Jesus, I know was there, and in fact prompted me in the first place. This, I now fully believe. What a comfort.

It was around about this stage in the whole tale that I was in the mall in Annapolis, not shopping, just wandering around aimlessly to be distracted by people and the world outside. A group of black female athletes, all in pink sweatshirts passed me and on their backs were the words "Have I not told you, be strong and courageous. Do not be terrified or discouraged, for I the Lord your God will be with you wherever you go." *Joshua 1.9*

God prompted me to contemplate what Dean meant to me, and what we meant to each other. He caused me to stand still until I recognized my own failings and foibles. God, who is Love, was there when I was terrified and discouraged, and promised never to leave or forsake me. And with the help of His Spirit I was seeing things more through His eyes and was ready to move on.

I knew Dean needed to know I was there by his side as always, that I loved him, and that we were in this great misfortune experience together. But don't think this was just for his benefit, it was equally for me. I needed to make myself talk to him gently, with no hint of martyrdom, which would have been so easy. I'm good at martyrdom sometimes.

When I think of Jesus' attitude towards those bosom buddies of His who were about to desert Him in the moment He needed their company the most. He was about to be arrested and crucified, and He knew that they were going to scatter away in fear. He comforted them, knowing they would feel awful and guilty later, and assured them lovingly of His presence with each of them always despite all their cowardice. Amazing.

"Do you finally believe? In fact, you're about to make a run for it – saving your own skins and abandoning me. But I'm not abandoned. The Father is with me. I've told you all this so that trusting me, you will be unshakeable and assured, deeply at peace. In this godless world you will continue to experience difficulties. But take heart! I have conquered the world." *John 16: 32-33*

No martyrdom here. Just gentle assurance and love. Jesus had unshakeable faith in God, His Father. What an example. And I bet His disciples thought back on that in the horrific days that followed. And I bet they wept a lot in the days and years to come when they thought back on the injustice of it all, the goodness of their Lord, their cowardice, and His humility and stoic love, and intent purpose for them and the world.

I could now weep.

I would curl up in that fetal position on the bed and weep, with the door shut. What do you say to God? I basically yearned to feel safe, secure, and looked after. Do I just ask Him to bring all the money back, somehow? I didn't do that. I didn't know what to ask or how to ask it. It was more just "Help me, help us, Jesus!"

**The Possible**

Several days went by where I truly eased up and we were able to rattle along peaceably. Slowly I realized my need to know exactly what had happened and how, and why. I wanted full disclosure from Dean who was finding the whole great misfortune unbearably difficult to face and talk about. I felt in the dark about our actual demise and needed it all out in the open – what had actually happened with our money? What did you do and why did you do it?

Of course, lurking around there was constantly the feelings of "How could he?" I'd hash them out to God in the dark, tossing back and forth, tears flowing. I knew I needed to be truthful in all this too, and lay out my honest, hurt feelings to Dean and to God just like Job. I felt newly free to lay it all out there. There were so many horrible people to forgive, and it was all completely unjust and unfair. Along with all this was the need for clarification. What had actually happened?

"Even if He slays me I will hope in Him; I will surely defend my ways to His face." *Job 13.15* I love Job!

And so, I told Deano that I needed to know everything step by step. He had to tell me slowly so that I got it straight and in logical order. I needed to know, so we could move forward in peace. I told him he was doing this for my benefit. Did the affects of a failed risk occur to him at all? The impact it would have on me, on our kids, on all our friends and community – did he think on those things? I desperately wanted to know he had.

Clearly and succinctly Dean quietly took me through the steps that lead to our great misfortune, steps that did put others ahead of us, in his attempts to save what turned out to be a lost cause. He found the whole telling difficult and embarrassing, but knew it was paramount that I got it straight because…

I was still holding onto a hurt. I was hurt not to be first in Dean's mind for protection. I felt disregarded and unimportant. That point, early on, where he had gone ahead despite my reluctance, and put our 'nest egg' out there as a possible lifeline to all the flailing investments. It was only later, on realizing the awful truth of our misfortune, that we had agreed together that it was more important to us that those who had invested through Dean 'got out' of any financial damage ahead of us. In my thinking at the time, anything to salvage face after that awful risk that my husband had taken!

So, quietly, without emotion or pointed fingers I asked Dean to talk to me about it all in language I could understand, and help me 'get' what had happened. I told him I thought he could help me process it properly so that we could both move forward as peacefully as possible.

So now, for the purpose of clarity, the dear man has again put it all in his own words for me here. He has read all that I have had to say and I know he 'gets' me, and my need to make this all straight between us. Generally speaking it's as he explained to me earlier, so genuine, open and honest. Yes there were tears but also lots of relief just to be back to openness.

DEAN: Well Nanny Poo, you have just written something of a love letter. I guess it is fair to say that I never really, properly twigged that you were so torn up; disappointed that I seemingly didn't put you first and, yes, I have to admit I kind of carried on not fully recognizing the pain I had put you through. Partly because I took your loyalty to me as a "given", indeed, I may have taken it for granted. And let's be honest, you are a pretty good actress and you, for my sake, disguised very well your hurt. I have now just read your account above with fresh eyes.

Here is what I can say. Over our, now, 49+ years of marriage, you and I have always played as a team. And over time we played very close in all the many and changing situations that we've been through; both the good and the bad. Neither of us would lord it over the other. But when a fork came in the road and a decision had to be taken, you allowed me to carry the deciding vote, even when we did not agree. Then you would back me and us as a team fully. You have always done that!

And that is what happened here. As the team leader for our finances, I over rode your request to not put all our eggs in one basket. But I did it anyway. And I did it because I was trying to take our financial future into a more secure setting in light of the collapsing stock market where we were heavily exposed. So I did that for us, but this time the investment was placed with people who lied about how they were running their company and I got taken, or should I say "we" got taken, but it was really me and you were my loving collateral damage.

You were so right in your description above. I was stunned when I discovered the perpetrators' foul play. I feared the worst for us, but I also was significantly concerned seeing the non-profit now exposed and I was the guy who recommended they put their money at risk too.

The effect that had on me was professional shame. That, coupled with envisaging you and me living shorter lives with more pain and less freedom. So there we were, tied to the tracks and the train, the inevitable train, was slowly coming to slice us up.

And yet, under those conditions, you stuck by me. And in so doing, once again, became my encourager and helped me see what we could do to fix the situation. You have always been rugged in suffering my enthusiasms. And there have been so many.

In this case, I felt really embarrassed to have been taken. It was an insult to my professional pride. Economics and finance is where I lived all my life and up to the fraud, the outcomes were successful. Now, like a doctor who misdiagnoses a family member; a civil engineer who screws up the foundations on his own house; a pilot who injures his family in a landing, or a marriage counselor that admits to being in a third marriage; the humiliation is all the more poignant. And in a way, isn't it often like that? The thing you pride yourself on seems to take the biggest hit.

But you were there to understand and encourage me. So when I saw the chance to legally pursue the criminals, I did, with your support. We knew it was going to be hard on us both and it would take a long time, and we never expected to get our money back. But we did persevere. And in the end, justice was served.

In the course of this long process, I have had to examine myself more than ever. Yes, with detailed witness interrogation from the FBI – always a cleansing process – it was a real dose of salts.

But more importantly, I was forced to swallow pride in buckets full and look with renewed humility to the love of God. When all materiality is taken away or was about to be, leaving us technically with more debts than assets to service them, and in our late sixties to boot, with less scope for digging out, here was I at a dead end of knowing how to materially cope. And you were depending on me.

But every morning we read the Bible together. We prayed together. We prayed as if everything depended upon it, because it did. There was nowhere else for us to turn. And we reflected. We had nearly five decades of shared experience together, you and me. And for all of that time, we both had trusted Jesus. We looked back on how he had guided us, provided for us, and blessed us with Emma and Jessica. Then kept on blessing us with the men that came into their lives and the men's families too. Then came the blessings of six curious and spirited grand children. And importantly, all families were intact and lived with good humor all around. And both of us have been given good health. So there was a basis for you and I to build on. We weren't done yet.

But the future at 3am always seemed the bleakest to me. I would wake up and immediately get hit with worry and dread. And it always seemed to happen about that time of morning. It still does sometimes, but less frequently and with less severity. And what did I learn? I learned that I as I woke up, I was worrying about the future because I saw it without Jesus. Realizing that, was a breakthrough! I think the idea was pointed out in the book, *The Shack.* Remember you really urged me to read it? And yes again, I was reluctant. I mean after all, it was, in my mind, a girls' book. And a husband resists being told by his wife what to read. But I am rambling. The key point is that when I began to thank Jesus on waking up in those dark early hours; thank him for the chance to trust him more, my perspective would change. The clouds lifted. And that is the nub of it for me, I think. Trust Him with my all; not just in my head.

For me, and I suppose for most rational people, the act of trusting needs to be well founded. It also needs to be experienced and hence, reinforced. And that is what our reflections enabled us to do when we started looking back in our morning readings.

But when things were smooth sailing, we did not grab hold of Him like we did when our financial assets were lost. As Richard Rohr has said, it is like "falling upward", a sheer belief that there is some kind of path that will be not just ok, but the best.

And why?

My basis for hope, and I know it is yours too, is Jesus' bodily resurrection.

The shorthand answer is because Jesus defeated evil by rising from the dead. What I mean by that is all that is good, all that is life itself, is from God. Evil exists to counter all that is good and that is represented ultimately by death and destruction and decay. Evil is a parasite on good.

So in rising from the dead, Jesus broke the reign of evil, thereby opening up the hope of restoration of all that is good. That, and nothing else, is my basis for hope and the basis for my trust in Him. And on that, He will lead us forward.

For you and me, what does that path look like? Plainly we do not know. In worldly terms, in actuarial terms, it more than likely means little or no recovery of lost assets. And at our age it probably means we will not be able to "earn our way out" like we used to. There is no room for a gospel laced with "material" reward. Jesus never promised that. He promised us the cross. To live close to Him and endure the pain that will inevitably come as our life in this fallen world progresses. The process of being refined by fire.

But what does open up is the fresh new appreciation of what it means to be alive. Through both what we often call "the good and the bad", we now look at events from a new perspective. It is from the hope that "all will be well and is well". Each day you and I wake up, as if standing on tiptoe, waiting expectantly, child-like. For example, what news will come in today about friends? Will there be reports of good career breaks or news of the return of cancer? Will there be more reported instances of evil and hatred like in our hometown of Christchurch; or will there be flat-out poignant examples of forgiveness, as at the Emanuel Church in Charleston, South Carolina?

Not to be glib, but without the burden of assets, we are more at liberty. We have more time to inquire, watch, examine, see love in action and celebrate things of beauty. And we can do that together now, more than at any other time in our lives!

And here is a funny example. When I was walking through a big-box store in Columbia, South Carolina last year where we were house sitting, the salesman leaped out at me to sell me a new television service: dish or cable. I thanked him, and said, "but I have no need because I don't have a tv." So naturally he wanted to sell me a tv for my house. But then I said, "But I have no house."

At least for me, it is freeing. But I know, dear Foof, you would love to have your own tiny house to spruce up and take pride in…just like you always have.

As for me, it is probably easier to live life without so many things around. Some boys are like that, as I always like to remind you.

I know I would never have taken that view of "imposed liberty" without being forced into it. Now, under the circumstances, I do find it rather refreshing. The "minimalist" life style is all the rage, for some. I think you and I experienced that in our early years of marriage. Certainly, by moving around so much, we found less was more. But now we experience that by the bucket full. And Jesus was right, less is more. But I would not have had the courage to take that step and find it out without the shove. But by being knocked off our horse, the belief and the ability to act on it moved from head to heart.

NAN: I remembered a comment that you, Deano, once made about yourself in a profile of some sort and it struck me then and even more now. You said you were a person who valued love, integrity, and friendship and resisted the temptation to distrust others. What did you really mean by that?

DEAN: A long time ago, my flat mates at university in New Zealand said I was overly trusting. At the time I'd lent the sum of about a year's university tuition to a Fijian student friend of mine. It was nearly all my savings. He was going to pay me back, but you know, he just never did. I waited. He told me he would pay me in Sydney as our ship docked at port. But he never showed up. By then you and I sailed out of Sydney and back to America, never to see or hear from Mr. Tuisuvivi again. But somehow, I do not feel bad about that. I trusted him, and he was in need. He let me down by not repaying. Maybe he is still trying to find me to repay. I do not know. That amount would have nearly paid for our combined sailing passage back to the America. Instead, we used your money - after you had worked nearly all year to save it up before we got married.

I do find it hard not to trust people. Somehow, by not trusting I feel I have made them less of a person. Then when they break the trust I become fairly disappointed in them. But if I start off by denying them the opportunity to demonstrate trustworthiness it is like killing the whole human experiment in love relationships, don't you think?

In contrast, the fraudsters who took our money set out to steal from the very start. At least that is what the 2013 FBI Press Release said. So this is a different matter. And it was evil. And as mentioned above, evil is a parasite on good. It exists and offends the sense of fairness that almost everyone recognizes anywhere in the world. And it has knock-on effects. It detracts and sometimes kills creative drive, which, in turn, stymies the development of our society. No justice means no trust upon which to take material risk. Hence no investment; and without it, economies remain stillborn and folks remain in their poverty. I have spent so much time in countries where there is little to no respect for the rule of law. In every case, poverty follows. In a fallen world, failure to protect general fairness is the root cause of poverty, hands down. I have seen it over and over again while working in many poor countries in the mission to help alleviate thier poverty.

So in business, you must begin with trust, but then through careful examination, verify the claims. Jesus calls us to be "wise as serpents but guileless as doves". In other words, "Trust, but verify."

NAN: I wondered if you had had any deeply thought out consideration of what your decision to go ahead and offer our funds would mean for me if all went south? Us. The girls. Our life in general. Why did you go ahead really?

DEAN: I was the board member of a large African Charitable Organization. They asked me to find a safe investment for them and after doing a lot of research, I recommended that they invest in what turned out to be this fraudulent organization. I felt keenly responsible and that was the reason I initiated the FBI investigation; fort he sake of recovery of money for them.

At this stage, I still remained hopeful that the business was reputable, but insisted that the Charity be repaid on time. So I persuaded them to refund some of my own money in order for me to try to use it to raise even more to help their business partially repay the Charity. Knowing that they had to keep me on side, they reluctantly agreed to refund some of our money, but they put strings on it, playing to my loyalty and integrity.

In order to do that, I had to decide whether to risk our own nest egg in order to get the others out first. And with that, I was putting their interest ahead of our own. It was a terrible position that the perpetrators put me in, but I think they knew that would be my response.

To make things worse, of course, in the end, the non-profit never even acknowledged my efforts over the six years in the FBI investigation, nor our personal loss which I incurred on their behalf. But you, the girls and I did experience the full and complete loss. That is why I said "in worldly terms" I should probably have kept the funds. But going into it at the time, I felt bound to protect the non-profit, even by putting our nest egg at risk. When it all failed, not only did the non-profit lose its money, but so did we.

I suppose this is hard for me to address because in hindsight I am pretty sure, that in worldly terms, I should have kept the money that was partially returned to me from the medical fraud perpetrators. If I had done that, we would not be where we are now.

As for these criminals who set up the fraudulent scheme, they are now in Federal Prison.

And as for me, I have been praying very regularly to have Jesus give me the correct view of their ultimate redemption and for me to forgive their evil acts. After all, I am supposed to seek what God seeks and that is the full restoration of a fallen cosmos, which he made and was deemed good. And it is right there in the middle of the Lord's Prayer: I must forgive as I have been forgiven. And so I do. And, might I say, as you do me.

As you know, I have been struggling with the loss of confidence in having been scammed. But day by day, you encouraged me to keep going. And it was you who saved our bacon by finding out how to house sit a way back in 2013 when we sold our house out from under us. And to this day, you are keeping us afloat by finding new house sitting jobs. That surely must be the subject of another fuller story.

Right now, as I write this paragraph, I am completely unable to see how the next day will develop. The next five years is a total mystery. But if the past five years is something to go by, you and I will find even more intensity in living. And by God's grace, we will be able to continue to bring brightness and light to all those other people we have not met yet. As well as bring encouragement to our kids, grandkids and network of friends who know our story.

NAN: I listened intently and thankfully. For the first time I clearly understood his thinking. I understood enough to remain calm and 'get it' essentially. I recognized that beautiful 'essence' of Dean coming through it all. That is the essence of him that I loved.

Funnily enough what came to mind were the many instances where I was absent as Dean made major decisions without me being present over the years. I have actually mentioned this as a point of interest when speaking to women's groups because those decisions of his would often make me upset and I would openly express loudly my disdain! It would be days, weeks, years, sometimes before I could smile and say "I'm so glad we did that." Our move to New Zealand with two preschoolers; our move to the North Island from Sumner (the girls' favorite place ever); buying at auction a house without selling the other one first in Wellington; Dean lying in bed with pneumonia and accepting a job with the World Bank Group. These subjects are all books in themselves! The fact of the matter is that we could never have predicted or dreamed the wonderful outcomes. Looking back I saw such truth in the saying that I have learned to take very personally "Nan, God's purpose prevails despite you, not because of you".

Here was a new situation where I was 'absent' in this decision regarding the great misfortune. In retrospect I could see that God does work everything together for good but sometimes in the process there are enormous hurts. Recognizing this allows hope to grow. There it was, alive in me. Hope.

I believe it was at that point, with fresh understanding and with those new eyes, yes, Jesus' eyes, that I forgave Dean's part in this horrible misfortune. And I had it clear and straight in my head why I had.

94

To this day, five years later, it is still unclear what any of the several victims' restitution situation is in the aftermath.

"Be gentle with one another, sensitive. Forgive one another as quickly and thoroughly as God in Christ forgave you." *Ephesians 4.32*

Forgiving quickly and thoroughly does not mean condoning what hurt me, or saying it is ok, or that it is forever forgotten, or anything like that. But it does mean accepting humbly my own part in the whole scenario, getting rid of that negativity that comes from any hurt, and so freeing myself up from that awful emotional baggage.

Ruth Graham, Billy Graham's wife, once said that marriage is the union of "two good forgivers". I love that. It indicates health and wellness of being; cobwebs cleared, and poison released. Heaven knows the number of times Dean has forgiven me very quickly for my temper, cutting tongue and outrage over what are often totally insignificant things. And, yes, my disinterest in his work!

Forgiveness is a choice, and ultimately it's for my own sake to free me up to live and to find ultimate value in moving forward, not dwelling stuck in the past.

Forgetting completely doesn't happen easily though. Those memories of hurt and blame dance around provocatively and start being bothersome. I read an article by Gil Mertz recently, which echoes a saying I've used in the past flippantly and now hold onto! "You can't change your thoughts with your feelings, but you can change your feelings with your thoughts"

It goes along with the life changing verse, "Don't live the way this world lives. Let your way of thinking be completely changed." *Romans 12.2*

Basically it means to change the way I think. "be transformed by the renewing of your mind" – an older translation. If that is possible, it will change the way I feel and ultimately the way I behave. But that change can only happen with the help of the Holy Spirit. I can't do it on my own. I know that. "Jesus, help me see Dean through new (your) eyes".

I love the way it's put in *The Message:*

"So here's what I want you to do, God helping you: Take your everyday life, ordinary life – your sleeping, eating, going to work, and walking around life – and place it before God as an offering. Embracing what God does for you is the best thing you can do for Him. Don't become so well adjusted to your culture that you fit into it without even thinking. Instead, fix your attention on God. You'll be changed from the inside out. Readily recognize what He wants from you, and quickly respond to it. Unlike the culture around you, always dragging you down to it's level of immaturity, God brings the best out of you, develops well formed maturity in you."

*Romans 12.1-2*

**The Impossible**

The final segment of St. Francis's statement is that 'suddenly you're doing the impossible'. Love is the key, and without love it is impossible to forgive from the heart and move forward. Moving forward was what I saw as impossible in those earlier dark filled days. But, once the necessary and possible things are accomplished, then the impossible can start happening. It's quite remarkable.

The 'impossible' is the Spirit given freedom now for me to see everything not just Dean, through different, poison-free, clear eyes. To be clichéd, it opens up a whole new world. Gil Mertz says, "Forgive your way to freedom." I like that.

In an intriguing way, by the act of forgiving, the many curious, obvious questions by us and by others are answered, but maybe not always as expected. It's because of a change of perspective. There's a paradigm shift which broadens everything. There's a different slant on all things.

Things like dealing with the physical loss of all our money and everything we owned. Of course it is frightening. Anxiety sometimes looms about old age, sickness, and what might happen out there in the future. But over the last 5 years, having stored everything we absolutely couldn't give up, in a 5x7 storage unit, which hardly ever gets opened, the concept of 'enough' has changed.

What is 'enough'? We've both slowly got the hang of 'Give us this day our daily bread'. He's never let us down. We're surviving with absolutely enough because, so far, we have all we need. Panic is seldom present.

I have always loved clothes, accessories, and quirky fashion. There are some wonderful thrift shops from Antioch, California to Columbia, South Carolina, to Canyon Lake, Texas, to Annapolis, Maryland, to Princeton, New Jersey. Ask me if you need directions. Thank God for the fashionable wealthy! I have not once felt 'drab'.

Dean is another story. His 2 sweaters, 6 t-shirts, 2 pairs of trousers, 2 shorts and 2 jeans travel around with us until he loses something, leaves it behind in the last house, or it falls off him with age.

Isolation from our friends and family is a feeling we battle. We strive to find some point of connection when we arrive in a new community, and that usually starts in a local church. How surprised we are, always, to find that necessary sense of "ah yes" through a great sermon, uplifting music, or good conversation with strangers who over time become friends. And thank God for the Internet which helps keep ties with loved ones. What on earth did people like us do years ago?

I guess you could say we've been 'stripped bare'. But to live in a home you don't own, using stuff that isn't yours, in a town you've never been to before; it does have a unique blessing all of its own. We can't possess or own or claim anything. There is nothing tying us down. There's a feeling of 'detachment'. Detachment from what? I think its ownership. Possessions. It's freed us up to get out and enjoy the awesome beauty, different in every place, all around us. Dean's photographs can vouch for the amazing sights and experiences we are enjoying. Although I often groan about the bike riding he drags me along on, I've got to admit biking is the best way to see, feel, hear and smell God's beautiful creation all around us.

Yes, reluctantly, we started out on an unexpected adventure together. Is it a 'reversal of fortune' in our almost 50 years of marriage? Well, maybe in a way, but with rolling eyes, laughter, and a lot of teasing we agree that we both own this crazy, intriguing story. It's a joint enterprise. The future is a phantom of which we have no knowledge, but God does. And so with His help, we endeavor to make the most of today, thankful to be together to face whatever comes next.

God is love. Love wins.

It is the key to genuine forgiveness, of ourselves and others. This frees us to live fully and joyfully in the moment:

> "May we experience this vast,
> Expansive, infinite, indestructible love
> that has been ours all along.
> May we discover that this love is as wide
> As the sky and as small as the cracks in
> Our hearts no one else knows about.
> And may we know
> deep in our bones,
> that love wins".

Rob Bell from *LOVE WINS*

# EPILOGUE

For about two months starting September 30th, 2013, we based ourselves in that house down the road from "Rangitata", slowly attempting to pull ourselves together. We would peep sideways into our old house every time we passed in the car, same side of the street, three doors down, which was about ten times a day. It was not easy, and felt like salt in a raw wound each time. Also, there we were carrying on in the community as usual. We could visit with friends, walk or bike all round the neighborhood, go to St. James services, and I remained in the choir. I would run into the same old neighbors in the brand new grocery store that everyone was so proud of. Everything was surreal. We were looking at everything through new eyes.

The one thing that made things a bit easier was the fact we were free to talk, but only when the subject naturally came up in conversation - we never meant it to be the focus. I guess it was so exhausting always explaining and dealing with awkward reactions, we trusted that the subject just wouldn't come up. And besides, who likes a whiner?

It was on one such occasion when it did come up, the Lord God proved Himself so profoundly to us, that we were literally gob smacked. It entailed a cup of coffee after an aerobics class with some of my old gym acquaintances who, apart from one, I only ever saw at the gym. The subject of our house sale came up and what were we going to do next? For the very first time I can remember, the tale of woe came pouring out like a torrent, amongst these women I hardly knew.

The result was extraordinary. Two of the women, within a day or so contacted me with offers of a place to stay. Just genuine, loving, concerned offers, one of which was so perfectly suitable for our needs, it still boggles my mind. It was an empty, ground-level apartment we could have until the whole house in two apartments sold. We would just pay our own utilities, could store all our belongings there, and it was just in the next neighborhood over from our old stomping ground on Chalk Point. It was in Deale, Maryland. And so we moved into the apartment for eight months, and started our new life, mysterious and far beyond our own understanding. But by March 2014 we were lifted into a whole new way of life – Long Term House Sitting.

In reality we had already been house sitting for about 9 months but now, suddenly, it became our option, our answer, and our saving grace.

We now like to think it's a sort of a profession. It's highly competitive and takes work. There's much paperwork, although all on line, to keep our profile, and references up to date. Each application requires us 'marketing' ourselves as the perfect fit for the homeowner. And then there are the photographs, which sadly need changing as the wrinkles deepen!

It was with a bit of research after learning what the word meant, that we found several registers we could join and then were completely surprised at what a sophisticated business house sitting is. We are not alone at all. There are hundreds of folks out there opting for this way of life. But maybe our reasons for pursuing this popular business are a little unusual compared to most.

House sitting, and how we came to choose this as the best option; our loves and hates about it; the secrets of how to do it well and get the very most out of it; and our facing of the still open ended conclusion to it all may come in another joint book which we fondly refer to as "The Reluctant House Sitter".

But now back to today. It is April 30th, 2019 and we are, if you recall, in our nineteenth housesitting job in Washington D.C. We carry on carrying on, but are 'morphing' into different people. We're still learning to live one day at a time; still yearning for the stability that all of us work for; and still continuing to wait and hope, endeavoring to live in the moment and choosing above all to trust God's timing.

> As in *Jesus Calling*, "Circumstances around you are undulating, and there are treacherous-looking waves in the distance. Fix your eyes on Me, the One who never changes. By the time those waves reach you, they will have shrunk to proportions of My design. I am always beside you, helping you face today's waves. The future is a phantom, seeking to spook you. Laugh at the future! Stay close to Me."

# APPENDIX:

## A SHORT PERIOD OF JOURNALING

For your interest I have included this short-lived spell of journaling. I started this while we lived in that above-mentioned first apartment for eight months. It'll give you a sense of 'real time' feelings, thoughts, trials, lessons learned, and our growth together of trust and thankfulness. You may find it a bit repetitive but I'll leave it here – you may choose to just scan or ignore completely.

Also it shows our growing realization of the love of God and how He works through the love of others towards us. The biggest lesson of all is on going - learning to accept his love through others by letting go of pride.

The journaling was short lived but, for me, played an important therapeutic part in this continuing adventure.

January 4th, 2014

Dean says to just start from now when I write. He's studied the 'art' of writing more than me and has produced some wonderful little publications including some of his beloved photographs, musings on childhood and prayers, all with the help of Debbie at the local Grauel's stationary store in Deale!  Deano's really on his way! His heart is truly in his work and the grandees love

103

his stories especially in the book "The Cry of the Cougar". I just write when I feel like it. I just get it all down, I guess.

Today the mood has been spurred by the fact it's Emma's 40th birthday – our 'firstborn' – and we sent her a card implying that the one good thing about her being 40 was that it wasn't 50! Hope she gets the joke! The relief is ours - that would give us 10 fewer years you see. It is not convenient this weekend to go up and see them and illness for all of us curbed getting together at Christmas so there's an element of sadness, and longing for family closeness in my tormented heart. Our spirited, noisy, fun grandees to enjoy and here we are – stuck.

Feeling detached and isolated is all part of an 'attack' Dean and I now face daily and have done for the last 2 1/2 years – the train is coming closer, we're tied, bound to those tracks like melodramatic Hollywood characters in the silent flicks years ago, floundering around, gaping wide eyed at the sight of the engine coming closer... closer! The need for normalcy can't be filled because nothing is normal any more and never will be again. Our lovely girls are aware of all this too and we hate to put them through it. At least now we can talk about things openly which we have been unable to do before now and so let me just get it down and start from now...

So, as of now, early 2014, our lovely home on the Chesapeake Bay is no longer ours – a place where we dreamed dreams and created a little piece of Heaven – 'Rangitata' – almost Heaven it means. It's Maori, and the name of the river my folks had our old fishing hut on in NZ. Dean and I named our home 'Rangitata' not having a clue what it meant and found out later googled it and it was so fitting as we felt we truly had 'arrived'. Not that we didn't work ourselves silly and spend lots of dollars outside and in to create just the ambience and atmosphere we craved.

I loved working with the sunlight, the colors, and woods inside, eventually finding the right spot for all the little eclectic bits and pieces collected from round the world, a mishmash of periods and styles, quirky, but everything with a story – I always remember a friend walking into one place we had and saying "well, can't say you're afraid of color or design – how interesting!" I never quite knew how to take her comment being new to the East Coast USA at the time, and hadn't quite 'adapted', and I'm inclined to adapt well usually – to my detriment, but that's another whole story.

Dean took on the garden with abandon. He happily went right back to his roots, taking time to dig, replenish the soil, research the right plants for the rather awkward area with its brackish water. Talk about transform and delight in it as he went. The joy! We would sit out in the many spots he developed for sitting and there were many, just wallowing in the expansive sights, the birds, the color, the grasses waving in the breeze. We'd sigh with delight and mutter, "Oh look, Nanny" "Oh Deano look how close the humming bird is---shhhhhh".

I found a poem in the *Washington Post* way back in 2004, just a year after we moved there, my eyes swelled up with tears at the perfect capturing of the scene, so I tucked it away. Emms loved calligraphy and copied it for him and he kept it in a lovely frame on his desk. 'Rangitata' for us was a 'gift' from the beginning.

A day so happy
Fog lifted early, I worked in the garden.
Hummingbirds were stopping over honeysuckle flowers.
There was no thing on earth I wanted to possess.
I knew no one worth my envying him.
Whatever evil I had suffered I forgot.
To think that once I was the same man did not embarrass me.

In my body I felt no pain.
When straightening up, I saw the blue sea and the sails.

*This poem was called: GIFT* by Czeslaw Milosz


And the light! The water surrounding us sparkled and rippled, leaving wavelets continually playing on the walls inside. Gulls, osprey, heron, geese winged their way across the vast expanse of sky back and forth into the marshes around us outside.

Never dull, always breathtaking even in the bleakest of winters when the river, completely iced over, played stage to the foxes, large and small – four of them, scampering across just yards from our bulkhead, teasing each other, rolling, and jumping with joy. It was so moving, and the perfect word picture to C.S. Lewis' comment "Joy is the business of Heaven" which we just happened to read this morning. There it was and is still. JOY, raw, all around 'Rangitata'. And we felt it and wallowed in it daily.

January 5th 2014

It is very cleansing to sit quiet and take stock of NOW. No tv, sold it and Ashkenazy playing 'Favored Chopin' behind this table as I sit over the one computer we share at present. I was always very 'blobby' in front of TV – when I think now, I wasted a lot of time just surfing mindlessly – some people have a lot more control than me – think my Dad must have read the same tendency in himself, so would not own a TV and therefore never gave himself the chance to test it. The tendency, I mean. There must have been something else he 'wasted' time on.

Our enforced break from 'Rangitata' has landed us in an unreal situation. It's a gift of another rather unusual sort, which came out of nowhere when absolutely necessary. This place is not our idea of 'heaven' at all, but we're making a painful effort to find reasons why we should see it as a gift. It's so easy to see it critically as a 'sock in the eye', as nothing about it is at all our idea of OK. I want sometimes to turn over in bed and not get up or see another day.

We were forced to leave 'Rangitata' and were forced to take what we could get for it. Finding our outlook very foggy, uncertain, and without the padding of any cash, we sold all we owned, delivered precious bits and pieces to the girls, and said "what's next"? I must say I'm so thankful for the attitude I was raised with "always be ready to give it up", or "you can't take it with you – hold it lightly". Something I rolled my eyes at years ago but now the wisdom of it rings in my ears constantly.

And so we find ourselves suddenly on the receiving end of "charity". It's hard to swallow – pride rears up and makes life almost unbearable. I don't want to go anywhere where the situation has to be explained and for a time we can't explain anything anyway – under orders not to – we've been "done over", defrauded, and feelings of helplessness, hopelessness, and being perpetually stunned rule my existence.

On top of this the sorrow for Dean and what he was going through – the horror of what had happened, and the knowledge that his heart was so heavy over what this had done to me. This was the point of "where do I look, where do we look for help"? I am learning slowly that until I give up and crumple up at the feet of the Creator, pride rules. Once I admit the need for help to Him I can more readily admit the need for help to others – it's the way God works.

And thus this 'gift', this apartment, through an angelic acquaintance who I barely know. She heard of our need, and offered, no questions asked. Have you seen the movie 'Frieda'? If you have you will glean a better understanding of this strange place than those who haven't This 'angel's' husband is a Spanish sculptor painter, wood worker and she, a real estate agent in this Deale area of the Chesapeake. She and I happen to attend the same exercise classes at the gym. There's a group of us there who enjoy each other's company and get together once a month for coffee after the work out. That's it. Don't see each other any other time.

At one of those coffees, when the FBI had alerted Dean they had at last indicted the 4 culprits of our dilemma and this was now public, suddenly we were free to talk. At that coffee I unloaded our situation, our need to sell the house, our lack of a plan for where to go, and the idea of house sitting for a while to gather ourselves together. The dear women were so receptive, aghast at the thought of being in the same fix themselves, and as a result two of them contacted me with the offer of either a room in their own place or, like this apartment, a space we could use.

Is God good? Yes! How dare we giggle at this place or complain! But we do! Numerous times now we have so enjoyed taking friends on a tour of the place in its entirety to laugh and gasp at it's, let's say "character". Raw wood, unfinished plaster walls, gaps, color scheme beyond belief, sculptures on every surface – bare torsos, lions heads, huge, covered with gilt, some very nice mantels surrounding not a fire place but a wall, Imelda Marcos type shoe closet, old, cheap fixtures in exotic, huge marble  bathrooms, at least 30 enormous garish metallic, paintings Frieda here screwed to the walls, multi metal chandeliers hanging everywhere.

The agent who sold our house came one evening with a great bottle of champagne as a Christmas gift and 'did the tour'. He has worked in movies and immediately, in awe, said what an amazing movie set it would make! We have freedom to be here till the house sells. It seems questionable if it will sell at all but then it only takes ONE buyer. There is one aspect that really appeals and that is that it's all rather fun. In the gloom of our predicament this is definitely a gift. The Lord has provided us with what we need for the meantime. I'm sure He has a smile on His face as he sees our mirth, but along with it he sees and understands our frustration of displacement. It's all so weird!

Very mindful that 'we have suffered a great evil', I feel surges of hate, resentment, envy, self-pity, insecurity, loss, desire to blame. And yet there's a drive, a resigned drive, to suck it up and keep going, it's going to be OK. I hold on to the memory of a desperate plea to God and his answer to me outside the Urology office, waiting for Dean in Annapolis. " Nan, calm down - I've got you covered". Looking out across the parking lot I saw in a row three tree trunks cypress, I think and to the eye it looked as if they had formed one huge umbrella cover. It was somehow just what I needed at the time and worthy of recall many times since. The strange thing was that when I drove up to the '3' trees they were now seven and all scattered about, not the neat 'trinity' I had spied miraculously before.

It's occurred to me that this is so typical of humdrum day to day life – things don't happen the way we expect or want most of the time and we have to breathe through our nose and say to ourselves there is something rich in what is happening right now and I'm going to try and look at this with a smile on my face even though I'm being eaten up inside. "Lord, please show me how."

I can't help chuckling at our current need to use our local library so to conserve gigabytes on our phones and computer. The library is our 'living room' almost every afternoon. The 'gift' in all this is that it is so close to the flat, and is warm and light – just a short bike ride away and somewhere to go. Dean takes his computer in and I use the library's along with a random group of locals who for some reason or another have to do the same thing as me.

I must say that with no TV and with ready access to books I'm reading a lot more but I'm not very selective. I like a variety and am engrossed in a high-tension mystery at present. Here's what the author had to say about libraries in the course of the story I was reading this morning which just cracked me up – it's so 'us'.

"The library itself does a bustling business, mostly with women bringing their young children in to look at books, but also the usual collection of homeless and elderly that a library gathers. It's a respectable destination. It's warm; you can be with other people. All the reasons why the Web cannot take the place of your branch library. Also it has books…"

From *"Blacklist"* by Sara Paretskys…and it was from my branch library!!

January 13th 2014

Gosh – it's a whole 8 days since writing – what has been going on. Not been that well, either of us, with a throat infection of some kind we seem to be passing to each other. Maybe the malaise over the last few days is due to antibiotics. Yes that's what it is.

For me just emotionally, I'm struggling to come to grips, yet again over the last 2 1/2 years this happens periodically, with what has actually happened, where am I to play my part in the scheme of things, and where to go from here as I wait for some sense of direction. I am so dependent on Dean, and always have been. I have always referred to myself as a 'kept woman' with a bit of a snigger but a sense of relief as well. I remember telling my mother on one of their visits to us in Bethesda several years ago that I "lived a charmed life and wondered how I'd react in a time of crisis having never had one".

The truth is that we have lost everything, everything, as a result of a complicated and very sophisticated fraud that I don't quite understand. All I know is we have nothing left. I know it was a trusting 'all our eggs in one basket' short-term investment, something I know in my limited understanding is never a good idea, and that is it really. We've been 'had' by a 'no good'. Here we are in our mid sixties starting out all over again like a couple of 20 year olds, floundering around and wondering where we go to from here?

There is a sense of guilt here as I realize this is my crisis as well as Dean's and I have a part to play whatever that is, in the outcome of it all. In a way when I married I really transferred my dependence on my father to a dependence on Dean, which was not really fair on Dean or me! I could blame my role model mother for installing in me this servant attitude, husband on a pedestal, just smile and be happy and often grit your teeth, but that's not fair on her either.

One thing instilled in me from birth has been a faith in God, that He has a plan and purpose for each of us, that we live by His grace, not our own efforts, yet we each have a role to play - our own special role, unique to us because we are 'beautifully and wonderfully made' by Him for that particular purpose. What the heck is that for me right now? I ran away from my last attempt a year ago – something I have been inclined to do all through my life. Always good with the excuses – I think it's insecurity somehow. What am I really good at that will help me right now to feel like I'm contributing to our efforts to get out of this mess...?

January 14th 2014

Went off to Pilates today – it's so good to get out, be amongst others, none of whom have a clue what I feel like inside. But then, who am I to make that judgment? Amongst our immediate gym group there are some really sorry situations and I wouldn't have a clue how they really feel. All I know is that going through this has shown me for the first time and from the most unexpected places, Christian love in action. Being on the receiving end is a strange feeling and something not easy to get used to. My immediate reaction is to decline with a smile – PRIDE!

January 16th 2014

Missed Pilates yesterday because I was so focused on a new idea. Having been stymied for weeks over what I, Nan, am to do in this no man land of the unknown, the fog, I have taken it to God night after night. I usually wake about 2am and am hit by the horror of everything. I mean we're NOT 20, we're from the first year of the baby boomers. We're old! Help! Where else to go but to the one who loves me, is all-powerful, all knowing, and all present? Never before have I felt so powerless and inadequate. There's nowhere else to go – is there? I love the verse in Joshua. *"Have I not commanded you, be strong and courageous, do not be terrified, do not be discouraged, for I the Lord your God will be with you where ever you go"* Joshua 1.9. My immediate thought is… "All very well…do I trust enough to keep going?" Those 2am wake ups, the darkness, the horrors grow, I see us scavenging in garbage cans, with our old wheel barrow holding not much, still together, still waiting for the answer to 'where from here'?

I have a bosom buddy, who knows me through and through, who rides this wave with me and plies me with wonderful books and words of wisdom all peppered with the most delicious humor and relief. Two years ago she sent our way *'Jesus Calling'* by Sarah Young. I firmly believe God sent that book to Dean and me through her to keep us sane, to remind us daily to re point our nose in His direction day by day and stick close trusting and thanking Him all the time, right through the problems we face, whether I feel Him there or not. Jesus warns us "If you work at sticking close to me you will benefit."

January 18th 2014

I have just switched on a wee string of white Christmas lights that we have hung around the large living room of this apartment so that we have some sense of twinkling light – to ease the closed in and cloistered sense we both have here. My bosom buddy, popped them in a care box at Christmas 3 boxes actually, amongst food and goodies to brighten us up. I love light. Light changes things, enhances things, brightens things, shows up things, causes shadows, it plays with everything around it. It's a gray windy Saturday morning and we twinkle in here. Went to the Dollar Store last night and bought $4 worth of candles for the kitchen table. God is smiling.

Dean went to Men's Breakfast at St. James and I finished putting together a Crockpot dish to simmer today for guests tonight but we don't know who they are yet. It's just the idea, just in case. You see, company lightens us up – there you go, an extension of 'light' again. Company broadens horizons, adds to the scene, gives us reason to care about someone else, provokes thoughts outside ourselves, enlightens us to other ideas and thus solidifies our own and so on. I am still hesitant at inviting – pride – because they'll have to sit on borrowed uncomfortable porch furniture, and our 5 glasses are all odd, and we only drink cheap wine. Where would we be without the Kyle's porch furniture which we're helping keep winterized! Truly – I know this attitude is entirely my problem – it's pathetic. It's inclined to determine who I want to ask and I hate that about myself. However, I'm ready for whoever it might be tonight and the aroma from the kitchen is divine. I'm organized and ready. Inclined to be happy only when I'm organized – love routine and structure – helps me think clearly. It's like the light can filter in and play. Otherwise everything is a jumble with no room even around the edges for light at all.

I've felt let down lately by the Lord because things aren't coming clear fast enough. Why is there no sign of things getting fixed? Suddenly I've remembered the words to me of a friend who has now passed on. You know that saying Mum used to fling at me often! "Don't just stand there – do something"? Well, this friend said when I first told her how foggy things seemed, "Nan, don't just do something, stand there."

This makes sense of a very sane little devotional book I found in Giant many years ago 'You're Late Again Lord' – the value of everything is 'in the wait' – although seeming to be standing still, the 'wait' is a verb and should be active, alert, expectant, trusting, anticipatory, ready for the next thing. However, it's all in His timing when He knows we're ready to 'do'. It's a sort of double entendre; we're in one place till…. But we're not to be dormant.

I am comforted to have realized that instead of just sitting and waiting for things to be the same as they used to be, I do expect something new is going to come, not the same but different, new, and it's not of my or our making, it's God's. To panic is stifling, blocking, unhelpful. I see clearly now that Deano and I have and are still endeavoring to be ready for the next thing for both and each of us. We sit shoulder to shoulder in bed every morning with a good strong cup of coffee made by whoever decides to get up and make it.

We read together a variety of helpful writings by folks we admire at present Daily Readings from C. S. Lewis compiled by Walter Hooper and called "*The Business of Heaven*", and also Sarah Young's "*Jesus*

*Calling"* for inspiration. Along with these we are reading through the New Testament. It is awe inspiring how the threads from each fit into the other writings – the order from chaos, the love of God for His creation, and we can know and see all this even through our trials. In fact it's the trials that teach us of our very necessary dependence on Him. We have to will in ourselves to grow the relationship we can have with Him because He would never force it on us. It's our own choice to know, learn, ponder, think, research and commune with the ever ready and loving Creator.

Then Dean and I just commit the day, pray hand in hand and shoulder to shoulder. We have learned to thank Him for the chance to trust Him more through this particular situation and ask what does He have for us today as we hit the floor. We both then swallow hard and face the day including the present dilemma.

Just two days ago I contemplated the last few months, thanked God for new clarity. We actually haven't stopped moving forward after all. I am ready now
to take another step…

Letter posted out January 16th 2014

Hi to good friends.

The new year is here and Dean and I have accomplished what we set out to do having sold our house - sold off our possessions, taken a much needed visit to family in Oregon/California, delivered precious bits and pieces to our daughters in Illinois and New York and reconnected with the grandees after what seemed a very lengthy separation.

It is now time to focus on the next little while as we seek direction. I have decided that the best plan of action for me is to offer what I know I do well, it takes no training, and I'm ready today. The reason I'm writing to you is that I only feel comfortable marketing myself by word of mouth, and you who know me are my best advocates! Could you just take a moment to read my 'blurb' and pass on the information to any person you come across who may benefit from what I've got to offer.

## NAN LEWIS OFFERS
## CONVIVIAL RESPITE CARE

I would like to offer some time to those of you who need a little respite, a deserved break from duties that tie you down in your home, be it with babies, children, or maybe ailing parents/spouse. I am not a nurse but I have an innate ability to raise spirits, be creative, or just be a gentle presence. On the other hand you may need shopping done or a driver to appointments etc.

I am in my mid sixties, active, fit, sensible and lively. I am a grandmother of 69yrs – 2yrs,
a wife of 44 years to my best friend, love music and good books, and am active in my church.

I have had some experience within the Hospice system of care.

We live in the Deale area and I have a clean driving record!

My rate: $15/hour
9-12am / 2-5pm Monday – Friday

January 22nd 2014

We've had a lot of snow over the last 2 days but are snug and warm and fine. I carried out my first assignment resulting from the above, yesterday, and it was satisfying, fun, and I hope will bring in a bit more work from the connection. Through a friend who received my 'blurb', she passed on the word to actually another acquaintance of mine whose mother needed help to get to an appointment etc. and so it goes. Got to be patient for more work but this will give me an ongoing arrangement every Tuesday. My charge is a character, very old, very on the ball, and great company.

I do have a penchant for the elderly, I think because I appreciate the wisdom that comes from the 'seasoned' set, though I must say the amount of wisdom varies from one to another. And I also love the challenge of raising their spirits.

Back when Mum and Dad were alive but ailing and Dean and I were flush with miles points and money, I would get home to NZ about every 5 months over a 3-year period and stay in Christchurch for about 6 weeks. The time was rich with just being with them, sitting out on the front verandah of 3 Elmwood Road with Dad in the sun he would often be much more lucid in those last years when he was in the sun, chatting about what took his fancy over our cup of tea. He was such a wise man always, and even as his dementia worsened wisdom would show up and often move me to tears.

We would take drives to their favorite haunts with a picnic. Part of my idea was always to give Ells a break, and I think I did, but there were precious times when all 4 of us Jimmy, Nozz and the 'girls' took off for the day to the Ashley Gorge or Diamond Harbor or maybe Akaroa. Ells and I took a plunge into the Waimakariri River on one such day and heard the chat between the 'olds' talking about us. "Look, there's a fat one and the thin one, and what nice girls." This all by Dad who was a bit unsure as to who we were, and Mum was just listening and agreeing but winking at us with her typical tongue in cheek grin. Hilarious!

I would come back to our home in Bethesda, Maryland and miss the texture and richness of these experiences. It lead me to search out ways I could add value to the day of the 'olds' in the neighborhood, or church, and I did a brief training stint with Hospice in respite care giving. But now it's different because I am compelled to ask for pay – I told my lovely charge yesterday how hard I found it to do that and she really put me in my place, told me of the need for my kind of care just in her area alone – wish the phone would ring!

January 23rd 2014

We drove through the snow last night to our neighbors round on our adored Chalk Point, after an unexpected dinner invitation. We drive by our house and peer in critically. They must have called a gardening crew in because it's suddenly all cleared, and they are only 'weekenders'. Hope they love it.

It was good to see the next door neighbors and catch up. They were our neighbors for the 10 years we lived at 'Rangitata', and actually the reason we even found it in the first place. It's funny how you can revisit places, people, and situations and for a brief moment it's as if nothing has happened – everything seems just as usual. But it isn't. The jolt of reality hits when returning to the 'Frieda' apartment with all its strangeness.

February 8th 2014

Well, weather of all sorts, ice, snow, freezing rain and here we are safe and sound. We've had an exquisite trip up to the grandees in NY and got everything back in perspective. I was quite convinced they had forgotten us, didn't care, and all those things that go with "loss". I think 'isolation' is the right word. It's the idea that no one else in the whole earth knows how we feel in our situation. But, I know that all we have lost is money, not the love of our lovely family.

Patience is something Dean and I pray for every morning. With patience comes help in not being so urgent wanting to change everything as fast as possible. Sort of a 'taking time to smell the roses even though they're hard to find' kind of thing! A friend opened up to me today about their situation, very similar to ours, how anxious they are, where to go from here etc. Our eyes were full of tears as we talked just so openly, honestly, and authentically about life. We talked about the importance of just taking things one step at a time. Trying not to project our sights out into the scary future where all you see is a mountain so huge and insurmountable that you just want to curl up and die.

And on February 7th, from Sara Young,

Come to me for rest and refreshment. The journey has been too much for you, and you are bone-weary. Do not be ashamed of your exhaustion. Instead, see it as an opportunity for Me to take charge of your life. Remember that I can fit everything into a pattern for good, including the things you wish were different. Start with where you are at this point in time and space, accepting that this is where I intend you to be. You will get through today one step, one moment at a time. Your main responsibility is to remain attentive to Me, letting Me guide you through the many choices along your pathway. This sounds like an easy assignment, but it is not. Your desire to live in My presence goes against the grain of "the world, the flesh, and the devil". Much of your weariness results from your constant battle against these opponents. However, you are on the path of My choosing, so do not give up! Hope in Me, for you will again praise Me for the help of My presence. Romans 8.28; Psalm 42.11

When Dean and I read this yesterday morning we just sat in silence knowing what the other was thinking.

This is for us today, right now. Thank you, Lord, for the chance to trust you more. I always remember my great Psychotherapist friend and advisor in New Zealand who said to me once that when everything seems hopeless, just take the next action you feel you need to take even cleaning the toilet, and put your focus and energy into it determined to do the best job you can. You end up with a feeling of satisfaction that the task is completed well. It's such a good point. Put your "all" into that moment and come out replete – forget that mountain ahead.

*"Don't worry, it may never happen"* was imprinted on a little Irish dish sitting above my family's kitchen sink as a child. What good advice from Jesus, a Psychotherapist, and an Irish dish!

It's hard not to feel out of it, disabled, knocked off our perch and totally displaced. Pride is raw and to suddenly be in a position of accepting "charity" is very threatening. I have realized through the love and care of others lately that this is the way God works – through others, His hands and feet. Christian love in action. It's the only way He can work.

Our mouths remain wide open in amazement at the care God has shown to us. Others around us are the means by which God proves His care. Sometimes it's so surprising coming from the most unexpected people, some of whom we don't even know. Hugs, outings, money, prayers, constant connection, friendly meals – and we sense no 'duty' in the outpourings, just love and care. All we can do is get down on our knees with thankful and humble hearts, and thank Him for them.

February 9th 2014

Well, little things are coming in to give us a boost financially. Dean pruned some trees yesterday, got a full body workout, and came home smiling and peppy. I talked to a second woman about some care giving for her mother and she will pay my gas – a big concern.

This afternoon I babysat for 4 hours! That's this week's food or my hairdresser money. I feel quite rich after that stint. My big aim is to get into independent living as soon as we see our way clear. Just a studio, even. My taste goes log cabin-wards. Thank you Lord for these dreamy nuggets. The time flew, by the way, not what I expected at all. I was on tap the whole time with a 5&3 year old, hyperactive little boys, grandchildren of good friends who just want to help us in any way they can. People genuinely care without being duty bound – it is so moving to us.

And, what's more, I enjoyed *Downton Abbey* in front of a roaring fire with glass of wine with another loving friend, along with the prospect of a repeat next week. What love.

February 11th 2014

We're sort of on a roll. Dean worked all day yesterday in the William's yard and cleared the pruned branches and limbs in 3 trailer loads our trailer owned with our neighbors to the dump. Now a neighbor of theirs is questioning who that guy is and could he do some stuff for him? I just see the Lord smiling and nodding as Deano comes home radiant, all flushed from the freezing out door air and hasn't thought once about the perps. A 'hump' has been flattened.

It takes a conscious decision to be transparent, willing to do anything, and grabbing the chances. Then, I think, we're in the correct position for divine guidance. It's very humbling indeed, but again kind of freeing. The Williams need help, one is in a wheel chair and the other is to have shoulder surgery. The garden is R's love, her therapy, and her life in a way. She is relieved; D. sees he can help Dean and me out; and he appreciates the relief from a huge bill. They all enjoy a bowl of soup and chat in between trailer loads. It's all so sensible. Thank you Lord.

I have just been offered a few hours work by a gym friend who runs an Ebay Assistance office just round the corner from this apartment. Would I be interested in a few hours a week doing some packing, labeling and mailing for her? My immediate thought is 'what has the world come to? – Me? Packing things?' The truth is yes, quite possibly, Nan. But I argue in my head that I can 'do' old ladies and be happy and chirpy and raise their spirits but where do my particular talents come in just packing things? There's no one to perform to, no company, just me packing things?

But – it does bare thinking about. A woman whose name I didn't even know has offered to help me out with a job in her office. She needs the help as she holds down three jobs, and I don't know what her situation is, but she is thinking of me, offering me help. What am I scoffing at? It bears thinking about seriously, humbly and thankfully. Also, it's so close to here. We do pray diligently each day for guidance, don't we? – Who am I to turn my nose up at the things that come my way without careful, prayerful thought?

I am about to go off to do 'a job' with an absolute character of a dear woman. I now spend time transporting to her Physiotherapy. It came about through my note to friends and I just love it. She has told someone else in her group about me and so it continues. Word of mouth is the way it works for us right now and it is so much more satisfying than sitting over a computer applying on line and not meeting one warm body in the process.

February 15th 2014

It's Saturday again and I have that familiar feeling of 'forget all the work of worrying and figuring things out and just relax'. I have spent most of the morning reading an historical novel from the library, thoroughly enjoying it. All about the Papacy and intrigues involved with it in the 15th century. A lot of sex, lies, and bluster. Dean has been at the St. James "Men's Breakfast" where his input is gratefully accepted and he loves the challenge of preparation and newfound knowledge to impart. Also, he loves the closeness to 'heart' things. He also takes over the teaching occasionally at a *"Bible for Dummies"* group on a Tuesday night.

Actually, it's been an answer to prayer – we've prayed for a move in the church towards a genuine interest in opening up the Scriptures and finding out what they actually say. And this study has been introduced. It's a great way to look at the Bible as a whole and learn what's there, why it's there and who put it there. I love the study for the clarifying of a lot of things biblical. There is no doubt that this time in my life is full of new, and probably necessary insights. I wonder what all this is leading up to? Fog, yes, but I must keep my hand in His and not be terrified. With God, all things are possible! He can do more than I would think to ask for or could possibly imagine. Sarah Young this morning.

February 16th 2014

Last night we decided to branch out and buy an antenna for our borrowed TV. I have to admit it's claustrophobic and kind of hard going constantly reaching into oblivion to find what it is we must be doing. A distraction is sometimes refreshing. Like TV. It turns out that we can only get 3 local channels bummer, but I have sat this afternoon with tears running down my cheeks watching on PBS the Morgan Choir Black, Baltimore singing "A Joyful Celebration". It was so needed and I am flabbergasted at God's personal awareness of my need. This amazing mass of black singers swaying and singing like angels the old spirituals I was so familiar with. I heard an amazing counter tenor backed by the choir singing several spirituals but what rocked me was his rendering of "Great is Thy Faithfulness". Memories of youth group camp grace before meals came flooding back, not that we sounded anything like them. But it's just the whole sentiment of security in God, the great Provider.

> Great is Thy faithfulness," O God my Father,
> There is no shadow of turning with Thee;
> Thou changest not, Thy compassions, they fail not
> As Thou hast been Thou forever wilt be.
>
> "Great is Thy faithfulness!"
> "Great is Thy faithfulness!"
> Morning by morning new mercies I see;
> All I have needed Thy hand hath provided-
> "Great is Thy faithfulness," Lord, unto me!
>
> Summer and winter, and springtime and harvest
> Sun, moon and stars in their courses above,
> Join with all nature in manifold witness
> To Thy great faithfulness, mercy and love.
>
> Pardon for sin and a peace that endureth,
> Thine own dear presence to cheer and to guide;
> Strength for today and bright hope for tomorrow,
> Blessings all mine with ten thousand beside!

I'm reminded life is all about thankfulness, automatically followed by trust.

With everything that plagues us at present another song that rendered me helplessly moved was "If I can help somebody as I pass along, then my living shall not be in vain". It just calmed me down as I think of the seeming piffling things I'm finding to do, like looking after old ladies. Suddenly I felt reassured that they're not piffling, they are what He has put in my way. "Jesus Calling" this morning, "Do not spoil these quiet hours by wishing them away, waiting impatiently to be active again…some of the greatest works in My Kingdom have been done from sick beds and prison cells or from the pits of enforced poverty – my input here! Instead of resenting your limitations, search for My way in the midst of these very circumstances…do not despise these simple ways of serving Me. Although you feel cut off from the activity of the world, your quiet trust makes a powerful statement in spiritual realms."

February 17th 2014

It was with a great deal of disappointment and yes bad temper, that I announced loudly that the antenna for the TV was not good enough as we could only get MPT, and I would return it. My thought was "boy we're really and truly in the pits", and I felt the clouds of a 'pity party' coming over me. I must say those clouds come over frequently but get warded off one way or another with wise words from my man, some shoulder to shoulder over the 'Word' and a good talk with the Creator and Knower of all things – perspective improves instantly until the next time. It's a continual bumpy journey.

However, back to the TV – I decided to leave it on yesterday afternoon on MPT1, and unexpectedly experienced the joy of the Morgan Choir. Over night, lying looking into space, I was struck by the fact that I've been supplied with all that I need for refreshment – MPT!

"That's all you need, Nan," He said. And I thought over last evening, lounging in a donated red leather arm chair even with it's own foot stool, in a rearranged living room, candles from the Dollar Store flickering, earphones on so I wouldn't disturb Deano at his desk and "Downton Abbey" – all 2 hours of it. And the prospect of my favorite British shows, cultural documentaries and all healthy stuff Daddy would approve. No politics to taint my mind and make me angry, nothing to roam around to mindlessly with the remote, just MPT – all I need. Daily Bread!

The week looks full of possibilities from this vantage point on a Monday morning. I start a new 2-day 2 hours a day, commitment with an elderly housebound lady in Crofton this week. Dean is interviewing in Rockville tomorrow with a big Insurance Company, having made the connection with a guy from church who genuinely wants to help. He has no idea what this means but you don't know till you go find out. Then on Wednesday comes an interview for the job of Executive Director, Deale Chamber of Commerce. What a hoot. We think it's funny and quaint that this would even be in the mix, but who knows? Only Him. We've learned too slowly that if we only entertain and carry out our own desires we sadly miss out on all that we, in our own puny selves could never see or possibly imagine. We need to be tiptoed, expectant, and ready for anything. What's necessary is constant prayer for His wisdom for discernment over all choices we make. Every moment is precious, don't waste it, or abuse it, or negate it. Put everything into it and enjoy.

February 18th 2014

Well, today I plucked very long hairs out of an elderly lady's chin and told her that I do the same thing to myself periodically. I played some beautiful songs on her electronic piano, singing to impress her as she was once a professional singer, and all that I heard through the atmosphere was her plaintive voice, "do you have any tweezers? I can't stand these bristles any longer".

## ABOUT THE AUTHOR


Nan tends to call herself an actress by passion, always loving center stage, musically and theatrically. It was a painful process being spiritually "honed", but eventually she found her true fulfillment, having to get herself out of the way and let God hold the audience in the palm of His hand. She learned this lesson while a Christian speaker for Creative Living International based in Potomac, Maryland and McLean, Virginia.

The author grew up in a Christian home in Christchurch, New Zealand and came to belief in her teens. At about the same time she took an AFS scholarship to a high school in Oregon, USA, met a boy who eventually followed her back to New Zealand, and they got married in Christchurch after both completing their undergrad degrees. From there they lived in Europe for six years, New Zealand for 13 more and then since 1991 in the Washington D.C. area. In all those locations Nan has been actively involved in music, drama and Christian groups.

She is happily married and has two married daughters and six grandchildren.

## COPYRIGHT PAGE